What We Choose to See

Our Notes on Cinema, AI and Communication

Acknowledgements

It feels almost surreal to be writing the acknowledgements for our third book. What began as a shared passion for writing and meaningful conversations has grown into a journey enriched by the encouragement, guidance, and support of so many people.

First and foremost, we extend our heartfelt gratitude to the editors of the newspapers, who believed in our ideas, gave our words a platform, and continually encouraged us to write. Their trust and support have been instrumental in bringing this book to life.

We are deeply grateful to our families and friends, whose unwavering belief in us has been our greatest source of strength.

Mr. Chaitanya Prasad would like to express his deepest appreciation to his wife, Ms. Shalini Prasad; his daughter, Ms. Bhavya D. Nandini; his son-in-law, Mr. Dhruv Kapoor; his mother; and his brother, Mr. Eklavya Prasad. Their constant encouragement, patience, love, and faith have sustained him throughout this journey.

Ms. Zoya Ahmad and Ms. Vaishnavie Srinivasan would like to extend their heartfelt thanks to their dear friends, Ms. Priya Kamra and Ms. Hansee Rawat, whose friendship, encouragement, and steadfast support have meant far more than words can express throughout this journey.

Ms. Zoya Ahmad is profoundly grateful to her sisters, Isha Ahmad and Ayaana ("Ana") Ahmad, for their unconditional love, encouragement, and constant belief in her.

Ms. Vaishnavie Srinivasan extends her heartfelt thanks to her parents, Ms. Subha and Mr. Srinivasan, and to her partner, Mr. Krishnan Iyer and his family, for their unwavering support, encouragement, and confidence in her every step of the way.

To everyone who has believed in us and our work, thank you for being a part of this journey. This book is as much yours as it is ours.

Preface

What We Choose to See is a simple title. Yet it asks a profoundly complex question.

Every generation inherits the same world, but no two generations see it in quite the same way. What changes is not merely technology or politics, but the lens through which we interpret them. Today, that lens is being shaped simultaneously by cinema, artificial intelligence and communication—three forces that influence not only what we know, but also what we believe, remember and ultimately choose to see.

Cinema has always been more than entertainment. It reflects our aspirations, preserves our histories, challenges our assumptions and quietly shapes our collective imagination. Artificial intelligence, meanwhile, is redefining how information is created, curated and consumed, raising questions that extend far beyond technology into ethics, governance, creativity and human agency. Communication remains the thread that binds these worlds together. It is through communication that ideas gain meaning, policies gain legitimacy, institutions build trust and societies negotiate change.

Although these themes may appear distinct, they are deeply interconnected. Stories influence technology, technology transforms communication, and communication, in turn, reshapes the stories societies tell about themselves. Understanding one increasingly requires understanding the others.

This book emerged from that realisation.

Many of the essays in these pages first appeared in the columns of *prominent newspapers*. They were written in response to contemporary events, evolving debates and moments that invited reflection. Yet as we revisited them, a larger pattern began to emerge. Beneath the immediacy of headlines lay enduring questions about perception, responsibility, innovation, culture and public discourse. Rather than presenting isolated commentaries, we sought to weave together a conversation about the forces that are quietly redefining our world.

The essays move across diverse landscapes. Some explore the changing language of cinema and the place of Indian storytelling on the global stage. Others examine the opportunities and dilemmas presented by artificial intelligence, particularly as India seeks to shape an inclusive, ethical and globally relevant AI ecosystem. Several reflect on diplomacy, governance, media, public communication and the power of narratives in influencing institutions and societies. While the subjects vary, the underlying inquiry remains constant: how do ideas travel, how do perceptions form, and what responsibilities accompany those who shape them?

Our intention has never been to provide definitive answers. The world is changing too rapidly for certainty to be a lasting companion. Instead, we hope these essays encourage readers to pause, question familiar assumptions and engage more thoughtfully with the transformations unfolding around them. In an age defined by abundant information but increasingly fragmented attention, thoughtful observation has become an act of responsibility.

As this is our third book together, it also marks another chapter in our own journey as writers. Over the years, our conversations have evolved, our perspectives have widened and our conviction has deepened that meaningful public discourse thrives when different disciplines are allowed to speak to one another. Cinema cannot be understood without culture, technology cannot be separated from society, and communication is most effective when it is grounded in empathy, clarity and purpose. This book is an attempt to bring these conversations into a shared space.

We are deeply conscious that every essay represents only one perspective among many. We invite readers not merely to agree or disagree with our arguments, but to continue the dialogue—to question, to reflect and perhaps to see familiar issues through a different lens. If these pages inspire conversations that extend beyond the final chapter, they will have fulfilled their purpose.

Ultimately, this book is about perception. About recognising that the world is rarely defined solely by what happens, but by how we understand it. In an era of relentless information, perhaps the greatest challenge before us is not learning to see more, but learning to see better.

We hope that these pages encourage exactly that.

Delhi Film Festival: A system in the making

Delhi has always been a city of stories. Political, cultural, deeply personal, something is always unfolding here. This March, cinema found its way back into that mix in a big way. The Delhi International Film Festival 2026 didn't just begin; it arrived with scale, energy, and a certain confidence that felt long overdue. For a city that once hosted the International Film Festival of India before it moved to Goa, this feels less like something new and more like something reclaimed.

But the real question isn't about how it started. It's about what it becomes. Because putting together a large festival is one thing. Building something that people take seriously year after year, that's where the real work begins. Right now, the festival has attention. It has curiosity. But what it needs next is identity, structure, and consistency.

If Delhi is to build a serious cinematic identity, the festival must resist becoming a one-off showcase. The first step towards institutionalisation lies in temporal discipline. The festival must anchor itself firmly to a fixed calendar window, a defined geography, and a stable identity. Just as Cannes is inseparable from May and Venice from late August, Delhi must claim its own moment in the cultural calendar. A late-March positioning works strategically, it avoids overlap with global heavyweights while aligning with India's academic and cultural cycles, but this must now be codified and protected. A festival that shifts in time and space each year risks losing not just recall, but relevance.

Once that foundation is in place, the next big shift has to be in how the festival programs itself. Right now, it feels like a wide, fairly inclusive mix, and that's understandable for a first edition. But going forward, it has to feel more intentional. Less like a collection, more like a point of view. The difference between a good festival and a great one is not how many films it shows, but how clearly it knows what it wants to say through them.

That means building sections that feel thought-through. Bringing in more director-led storytelling, where the craft and perspective matter as much as the narrative itself. Giving real, central space to women-directed and women-centric cinema, not as a token category, but as a core part of the programming. And also leaning into films that engage with real, lived issues, social, political, environmental. Because the festivals that stay with you are the ones that reflect the moment you're living in.

At the same time, Delhi has the opportunity to do something most festivals in India haven't fully managed yet, to become a space where cinema is not just screened, but developed. There is so much raw talent in this city, students, theatre actors, independent creators, people experimenting with storytelling in ways that don't always find platforms. The festival can step into that gap. Script labs, pitching forums, casting platforms, youth sections, these aren't add-ons, they're what can make the festival feel alive beyond the screenings.

What can really set Delhi apart, though, is how deeply it involves its own people. Right now, a lot of the festival still sits within designated venues. But cinema has the ability to move, to travel, to meet people where they are. Open-air screenings across neighbourhoods, community-led programming, student participation, and these things can turn the festival into something the city feels a part of, not just something happening around it. The more people feel included, the stronger the festival becomes. There's also a strong case for going deeper within India itself.

If the festival wants to be global, it has to first be rooted. Regional cinema needs more than representation; it needs prominence. Voices from the

North-East, independent filmmakers, and smaller industries, they should feel central, not peripheral. And alongside that, OTT can't be ignored. It's not a parallel world anymore; it's part of the same ecosystem. Bringing it into the festival, giving it space, engaging with it seriously, that's just being honest about where cinema is today.

At the same time, the global cinema showcase this year has been one of the festival's strongest signals of intent. Bringing films from across continents, diverse storytelling styles, and different cinematic languages onto one platform has helped position Delhi as outward-looking and internationally aware. The current edition has seen a notable focus on regions such as Saudi Arabia and parts of Africa, alongside a wider mix of international entries from Europe, Asia, and beyond. But going forward, this needs to become sharper and more curated. Instead of broad representation, the festival could move towards focused country spotlights, director retrospectives, and region-specific showcases that offer deeper engagement rather than surface-level exposure. Building sustained partnerships with global festivals and film bodies can also ensure that Delhi is not just screening international cinema but becoming part of its circulation. The goal should be to move from access to influence.

If Delhi really wants to move into the league of major festivals, it also needs to think beyond screenings and build an industry layer. Spaces where filmmakers meet producers, where ideas find backing, where collaborations begin. That's what gives a festival weight. And in doing so, it doesn't have to compete with the International Film Festival of India. It can actually complement it, where IFFI remains the flagship, Delhi can become more agile, more industry-facing, and more experimental.

A lot of this, of course, depends on how the government chooses to take this forward. Not just as an annual event to organise, but as something to build over time. That means consistency in funding, long-term thinking, and a structure that exists beyond individual editions. Because festivals like this don't become important overnight, they grow into that space.

Right now, the Delhi International Film Festival has done something important: it has made people look. It has been shown that Delhi can host something of this scale and do it well. But attention doesn't last. What lasts is substance.

The next edition doesn't need to be bigger. It just needs to be clearer. More confident about what it stands for and where it wants to go.

Because if Delhi gets this right, it won't just be another stop on the festival circuit. It will become a place where cinema actually feels like it belongs.

The tsunami of 2026: How Dhurandhar brought audiences flooding back to theatres

There was a time, not too long ago, when it genuinely felt like the cinema hall was becoming irrelevant. Streaming had taken over convenience, attention spans had shortened, and the ritual of going to the movies seemed almost... nostalgic. Something you did before life got faster, smaller, more screen-sized.

And then Dhurandhar happened. Not quietly. Not gradually. But like a full-blown cultural jolt.

What we're witnessing in 2026 isn't just the success of a film. It's a phenomenon, almost a collective remembering. The kind where audiences aren't just watching a movie, they're returning to something they didn't realise they had missed this deeply.

If you've seen the visuals, packed theatres, people lining up hours in advance, fans celebrating outside cinemas, you know exactly what this feels like. It's not just footfall; its emotion spilling into public space. "First Day First Show" used to be a badge of honour. With Dhurandhar, it has become a movement again. There's something electric about sitting in a dark hall, surrounded by strangers who are reacting with you. The whistles, the gasps, the applause, it's chaotic, loud, and completely alive. No living room, no matter how high-end your setup is, can replicate that shared adrenaline. And Dhurandhar 2 is riding that wave with full awareness. This time, the audience isn't just curious, they're waiting. Anticipating. Almost rehearsing their return.

Why Dhurandhar Worked (And Why the Sequel Will Too) Let's be honest, hype alone doesn't create a tsunami. Plenty of films open big and disappear just as quickly. What Dhurandhar got right was deceptively simple: it respected the audience's intelligence while still delivering spectacle. It wasn't trying to be clever for the sake of it, nor was it relying purely on scale. It struck that rare balance, strong storytelling, memorable characters, and moments that were designed for the big screen.

And that last part matters more than we often admit. Some films can survive on OTT. Dhurandhar demanded a theatre. Wide frames, sound design that hits your chest, sequences that feel incomplete on a smaller screen, this is cinema built for immersion. Once audiences experienced that, it reset expectations. So when Dhurandhar 2 comes in, it's not starting from zero. It's building on trust. The audience already believes this world is worth returning to. Sequels, when done right, aren't just continuations, they're invitations. And here, the invitation is clear: come back, it's going to be bigger, louder, and worth your time again.

Is This a One-Off, or Something Bigger? That's the more interesting question. Because if this was just about one film, we wouldn't be seeing the ripple effects elsewhere.

The re-release culture, for instance, is telling us something important. Classics returning to theatres, and filling seats, is not just nostalgia. It's proof that audiences are craving the experience, not just the content.People aren't just going to watch a film they've already seen. They're going to feel it again, but this time, collectively.

Similarly, the success of sequels and franchise continuations isn't just about brand value. It's about emotional continuity. Audiences want to revisit worlds they've already invested in, but they want to do it in a space that amplifies that connection. The theatre does that.

Maybe this resurgence is also about something more human. After years of isolation, personal screens, and fragmented attention, there's a quiet hunger for shared experiences. Not curated, not algorithm-driven, but spontaneous, collective, and a little unpredictable. Cinema halls offer that. You don't control the reactions around you. You absorb them. And in doing so, the film becomes bigger than itself. That's what Dhurandhar tapped into, perhaps unintentionally, but effectively. It reminded people that movies are not just stories. They're events.

What makes this moment even more fascinating is how cinema is quietly reclaiming its place as a social ritual. For a long time, entertainment became increasingly individual: your phone, your headphones, your algorithm. Even when we watched the same shows, we watched them alone. The theatre disrupts that isolation. With Dhurandhar, people didn't just attend screenings, they planned them. Group bookings, late-night shows, repeat viewings with different friends. It almost feels like going to the movies has become an occasion again, not just an activity you squeeze into your day.

And that shift matters. Because when something becomes an occasion, it automatically gains value. You dress up for it, you make time for it, you talk about it afterwards. The film extends beyond its runtime, it becomes part of conversations, memes, and shared memory.

There's also an interesting recalibration of what "star power" means in this moment. Earlier, stars alone could pull audiences to theatres. Then came a phase where even big names couldn't guarantee footfall. But now, with films like Dhurandhar, it feels like star power has evolved; it's no longer just about who is on screen, but what the film promises. The actor, the director, the music, the visual scale, they all come together to create a sense of inevitability. A feeling that this is something you cannot miss in theatres.

And once that perception is established, audiences respond instantly.

What Dhurandhar and its sequel are ultimately doing is setting a new benchmark, not just commercially, but experientially. It's no longer enough for a film to be "good." It has to justify the decision to step out, buy a ticket, and sit in a theatre with strangers. It has to offer something that cannot be replicated at home. That's a higher bar, but also a more exciting one. Because if this trend continues, we might be entering a phase where filmmakers start designing cinema for the theatre first again, instead of treating it as just one of many distribution platforms.

And maybe that's the real story here. Not just that audiences are coming back, but that cinema is slowly reclaiming its original promise. A place where stories aren't just watched, but felt together.

Calling this a "tsunami" isn't an exaggeration. It's a shift in behaviour. Audiences are showing up again, not just for content, but for connection. For scale. For that fleeting, unrepeatable energy that only exists when hundreds of people are watching the same moment unfold together. Dhurandhar 2 is poised to amplify this even further. Because now, it's not just a film release. It's a continuation of a feeling people don't want to lose again.

If there's one takeaway from all of this, it's this: The cinema-going experience was never dead. It was waiting for the right trigger. Dhurandhar happened to be that trigger.

And if filmmakers understand what truly brought audiences back, not just scale, not just hype, but the promise of an experience worth leaving home for, this resurgence might not just last. It might redefine what success in cinema looks like again. Because at the end of the day, people don't just want to watch movies. They want to go to the movies.

Communication ethics in an age of conflict

In today's media environment, wars rarely remain confined to battlefields. They unfold just as vividly on television screens, digital platforms, and social media timelines. Every strike, every explosion, every movement of troops travels across the world within seconds. Technology has made it possible for audiences thousands of miles away to witness conflict almost as it happens. Yet this unprecedented access has created a strange paradox: the more we see of war, the less we often understand it.

What we are witnessing is the emergence of a new communication order around conflict. Information moves at extraordinary speed, but reflection rarely keeps pace with it. Images circulate faster than context. Algorithms amplify the most dramatic footage, and broadcasters compete for attention in an increasingly crowded media landscape. In such a setting, communication itself becomes part of the battlefield. While military operations determine the physical outcomes of war, the information environment shapes how societies interpret those events, how they emotionally respond to them, and sometimes even how they participate in them.

War reporting has not always looked like this. For most of the twentieth century, there was a distance between the battlefield and the newsroom. Journalists filed reports after verifying what had happened, often hours or even days later. That delay, though frustrating at times, created space for editorial judgment and context. Stories were written with the benefit of reflection rather than immediate reaction. Today, that distance has almost disappeared. Twenty-four-hour news cycles and real-time satellite feeds have transformed war into something that resembles a continuous broadcast event. The shift is subtle but important: we are no longer only reporting war, we are broadcasting it.

Television studios increasingly resemble control rooms for a global spectacle. Large digital screens display animated maps, missile trajectories, and radar simulations. Footage of explosions is replayed repeatedly from multiple angles. Anchors narrate unfolding events with urgency and drama. Graphics and sound design sometimes mirror the visual language of cinema or sports broadcasting.

In this environment, visual intensity often replaces informational depth. The purpose quietly shifts from explaining events to capturing attention. Ratings, viewership metrics, and digital engagement begin to shape editorial decisions. War becomes a form of content.

This raises an uncomfortable but necessary question: when conflict is presented as spectacle, does the audience gradually become a spectator rather than an informed citizen?

Images, of course, have always played an important role in communication. Powerful visuals can humanise distant suffering and generate empathy across borders. They can make the consequences of war visible in ways that statistics never could. But images also have the power to distort reality when they are presented without context.

In contemporary conflict coverage, viewers often encounter an endless loop of explosions, missile launches, and night-vision footage. Cameras gravitate toward the most dramatic scenes, fireballs lighting up the sky, buildings collapsing under airstrikes, or tracer rounds cutting through darkness. What receives far less attention are the quieter and slower dimensions of war: displaced families, fragile diplomatic negotiations, economic disruptions, or the long and complicated process of rebuilding societies after violence.

The result is a kind of visual hierarchy of war. The most spectacular moment dominates the narrative, while the structural realities that explain conflict remain largely invisible. Audiences are exposed to bursts of violence but rarely to the deeper political, historical, and economic contexts that led to the conflict in the first place.

Over time, this can produce something even more troubling: normalisation. When viewers encounter dramatic imagery of violence day after day, war can begin to resemble a form of high-stakes entertainment rather than what it truly is, a catastrophic breakdown of political order.

A newer challenge is now intensifying this dynamic: the growing use of artificial intelligence in visualising conflict. Some broadcasters have begun using AI-generated imagery or digital simulations to reconstruct how an attack might have unfolded, how missiles may have travelled, or how military planners might have executed a particular operation. These visualisations are often presented as explanatory tools, but they occupy a complicated space between journalism and dramatisation. Even when clearly labelled as simulations, the realism of AI-generated imagery can blur the boundary between fact and speculation. For many viewers, the difference between a verified image and a reconstructed scene may not always be obvious.

More importantly, such simulations often prioritise visual drama over analytical clarity. Stylised animations of military operations risk turning strategic violence into something resembling a cinematic sequence. What is presented as explanation can easily slip into oversimplification, or worse, a kind of theatrical staging of conflict. In an era already struggling with misinformation and manipulated media, the casual use of such imagery deserves far more scrutiny than it currently receives.

At its core, the issue is not technological but ethical. Media institutions across the world have developed elaborate codes of conduct for elections, political reporting, and even public health crises. Yet when it comes to the communication of war, reflection often gives way to speed.

Several uncomfortable questions, therefore, remain insufficiently discussed. Should broadcasters repeatedly display the mechanics of weapons used in attacks? Does visualising military capabilities inadvertently glorify violence or reveal sensitive information? How much speculative reconstruction should be permitted in news coverage? And perhaps most importantly, at what point does reporting cross the line into dramatisation?

These are not minor editorial dilemmas. They point to a deeper problem within the global communication environment: communication itself rarely undergoes introspection during conflict. The urgency of reporting tends to overshadow the responsibility of representation.

Perhaps it is time to think about a clearer ethical boundary. In sports, certain violations are so serious that they trigger an immediate red card. It is a simple but powerful signal that a line has been crossed. Everyone understands the rule, and everyone understands the consequence.

Conflict communication might benefit from something similar, a conceptual "red card" for media ethics. Such a framework would not exist to censor reporting but to establish limits that protect the integrity of journalism. Certain practices could clearly fall into this category: presenting speculative military scenarios as factual visuals, repeatedly looping violent imagery purely for dramatic effect, revealing tactical details that may escalate tensions, using AI-generated visuals without clear disclosure, or framing conflict in ways that trivialise human suffering. The goal would not be to silence journalism but to recalibrate it. Because the media ecosystem today is global, such questions cannot be addressed by individual broadcasters alone. A broader conversation is needed among international journalism bodies, academic institutions, and organisations concerned with information ethics. Together, they could help articulate a set of shared principles for responsible conflict communication.

Such principles might begin with a simple but important idea: context should always come before spectacle.

Historical background, diplomatic developments, and humanitarian consequences should accompany battlefield imagery. Audiences deserve to understand not just what is happening, but why it is happening.

Transparency should also guide the use of digital reconstructions and AI simulations. If such visuals are used, they must be clearly labelled and treated as illustrations rather than evidence. At the same time, the human cost of war must be represented with the same prominence as military developments. Civilian suffering, displacement, and long-term societal damage are not side stories; they are central to the reality of conflict. Editors should also be mindful of how visual repetition shapes perception. Endless loops of violent imagery may attract attention, but they can also desensitise audiences and distort understanding. And in the relentless race to break news first, verification must never become secondary to speed.

Ultimately, the question is not whether wars will continue to be reported in real time. That is inevitable. The more important question is how societies choose to communicate war.

Media institutions hold immense power in shaping public perception. Their narratives influence how people interpret global events, how governments respond to crises, and how societies emotionally process conflict. Communication can inflame tensions and amplify fear, but it can also foster understanding and restraint.

The emerging communication order around war therefore, demands more than technological sophistication. It requires moral imagination. The ability to broadcast instantly must be matched by the wisdom to decide what should be broadcast, and how it should be presented.

In a world where war can be watched live from living rooms across continents, communication carries an enormous responsibility. Journalism must resist the temptation to turn conflict into spectacle. Its task is not to amplify the noise of war, but to illuminate its meaning.

MANAV: The civilisational blueprint for the age of artificial intelligence

In February 2026, New Delhi did not merely host a technology conference. It staged a civilisational argument. At the

India AI Impact Summit, global policymakers, scientists, entrepreneurs, ethicists, and diplomats did not gather to debate artificial intelligence as a tool; they gathered to confront a question that will define the century: What kind of intelligence should shape humanity's future?

What emerged from Bharat Mandapam was not another declaration of innovation supremacy or a race for computational dominance. Instead, the world witnessed the articulation of a philosophical architecture for AI, Prime Minister Narendra Modi's MANAV doctrine, a framework that reframes artificial intelligence not as an industry, but as a moral project.

For over a decade, global AI discourse has been shaped largely by two poles: technological accelerationism and regulatory anxiety. One celebrated scale and speed; the other feared loss of control. The India AI Impact Summit reframed the conversation entirely. It proposed that the real debate is neither speed nor restraint, but purpose.

Observers across continents noted a striking shift. Delegates did not leave speaking about India's infrastructure or markets alone. They left speaking India's language of AI: ethics, inclusion, sovereignty, trust, and public good. In diplomatic corridors afterward, a quiet consensus began to form: India had introduced not a policy stance, but a vocabulary. And vocabulary is power. Whoever defines the terms of a global conversation shapes its trajectory.

The acronym MANAV, Moral systems, Accountable governance, National sovereignty, Accessible AI, Valid systems; may appear administrative at first glance. In reality, it is architectural. It reorganises how nations conceptualise intelligence systems and their place in society.

India's insistence that fairness, transparency, and human oversight be embedded into AI from the classroom upward signals a long, term strategy. Ethical literacy is being cultivated as a civic skill, not a technical afterthought. The Guinness World Record pledge campaign, nearly a quarter, million commitments in 24 hours, demonstrated that responsible AI can become a participatory movement rather than an elite debate.

Where many nations treat regulation as a brake, India treats it as a foundation. TheINR 10,300, crore IndiaAI Mission embeds oversight into compute access, model deployment, and public, sector usage. This signals to the world that trust is not the enemy of innovation; it is its multiplier.

In the AI age, sovereignty is measured not only in territory but in data, algorithms, and chips. India's push for domestic compute capacity, semiconductor manufacturing, and secure datasets reflects a doctrine of open collaboration with strategic independence, a model increasingly attractive to middle powers wary of technological dependency.

India's Digital Public Infrastructure, shared compute portals, dataset repositories, and supercomputing networks redefine access economics. By lowering barriers for startups, students, and researchers, India positions AI not as a luxury resource but as a public utility. The message resonated strongly across the Global South: technological progress need not deepen inequality. At a time when deepfakes threaten elections and synthetic media blurs truth, India's regulatory definition of AI, generated content and investment in auditing tools signal a decisive stance: legitimacy must be engineered, not assumed. This transforms trust from a philosophical concept into a technical specification. The summit compelled global observers to recognise three realities about India's AI trajectory: First, India is not attempting to replicate Silicon Valley or Shenzhen. It is building a third model, civilisational AI, where technology development is aligned with democratic norms, pluralism, and public welfare.

Second, scale can be ethical. With one, sixth of humanity, India's ability to implement inclusive digital infrastructure at population scale demonstrates that mass adoption and moral safeguards are not mutually exclusive. Third, AI leadership is no longer defined solely by patents or compute clusters. It is defined by narrative authority. By presenting a coherent moral framework, India positioned itself as a thought leader in shaping how the world thinks about intelligence itself.

Historically, nations influenced the world through culture, trade, or military power. In the 21st century, influence increasingly flows through technological norms. Just as global finance once adopted Western regulatory standards and international diplomacy adopted UN vocabulary, AI governance is now entering a phase where conceptual frameworks will standardise globally.

The Delhi summit suggested that India's vocabulary may become that standard.

Already, policymakers from multiple regions are studying India's AI governance guidelines, public compute models, and ethical frameworks as templates adaptable to their own contexts. What makes the Indian approach persuasive is not rhetoric but replicability. It is designed for countries that lack billion, dollar labs but possess human capital and ambition.

The genius of the MANAV vision lies in its universality. It is culturally rooted yet globally legible. Its principles, ethics, accountability, sovereignty, accessibility, legitimacy, are values every society recognises, regardless of political system or technological maturity. This universality transforms MANAV from a national doctrine into a potential global charter. Much like the concept of sustainable development moved from environmental discourse into economic policy worldwide, human, centric AI may follow a similar path, originating in India but adopted internationally.

Summits often produce declarations that fade into archives. This one produced alignment. Delegates departed not with communiqués but with frameworks, datasets, partnerships, and shared language. The conversations begun in New Delhi are already extending into bilateral agreements, academic collaborations, and startup ecosystems. In diplomatic terms, the summit functioned as a signalling event. It told the world that India is not waiting to participate in the AI future, it is helping write its operating principles. If the 2010s were defined by the question "Who builds AI?" the 2030s may be defined by "Whose principles guide AI?"

India's bet is clear: technological leadership will belong not to the fastest innovator, but to the most trusted one. Nations, companies, and citizens will gravitate toward systems they believe are fair, explainable, and accountable. By institutionalising those qualities early,

India is positioning itself as the reference model for trustworthy intelligence.

The long, term implication is profound. As global standards bodies, academic institutions, and regulatory alliances begin adopting similar principles, India's framework could quietly become the grammar of global AI governance. The deepest takeaway from the India AI Impact Summit is philosophical. Artificial intelligence is often discussed as a frontier. India framed it as a mirror. Technology reflects the values of those who build it. If that reflection is distorted, society fractures. If it is balanced, society advances.

Through MANAV, India has proposed that the future of intelligence must remain anchored in humanity. Not human versus machine, but human guiding machine. That is why the summit will likely be remembered not as an event, but as a turning point: the moment the world realised that the next chapter of artificial intelligence might not be written only in code, but in conscience.

India as Global South's voice in Artificial Intelligence

at the India AI Impact Summit 2026

As artificial intelligence transitions from technological novelty to economic necessity, a fundamental question confronts the international community: whose values will shape its development, and who will benefit from its transformative power? The ongoing India AI Impact Summit 2026, at New Delhi, has emerged as a deliberate answer positioning emerging economies not as passive recipients of technology, but as active architects of an AI-driven future. The AI mantra narrative is everywhere.

This gathering represents far more than another conference on emerging technologies. It signals India's strategic ambition to reframe artificial intelligence through the lens of developing nations. At its heart lies a philosophy rooted in the Indian philosophy of "Vasudhaiva Kutumbakam"— the world as one family reimagined for the digital age as JanAI, or AI for the people. It marks the next major milestone for India following its G20 presidency in 2023.

The timing of this summit carries particular significance. With AI markets expanding rapidly across developing regions and India's own sector projected to exceed seventeen billion dollars by 2027, New Delhi seeks to establish itself as more than a technology consumer. The country aims to become the conceptual bridge between cutting-edge innovation and meaningful societal transformation, particularly for nations often marginalised in technology governance discussions.

India's approach rests on three foundational principles which organisers term "Sutras"— that prioritise people, environmental sustainability, and comprehensive progress. These pillars reflect a conscious departure from AI development models focused primarily on commercial velocity or geopolitical advantage. Instead, they acknowledge the complex realities facing developing nations: limited infrastructure, diverse linguistic landscapes, vast rural populations, and pressing developmental challenges that technology must address rather than exacerbate.

Translating broad philosophy into tangible outcomes, summit organisers have identified seven interconnected domains of cooperation, termed "Chakras" in reference to centers of energy and focus. These areas-spanning human capacity building, social inclusion, trustworthy AI systems, institutional resilience, scientific advancement, resource democratisation, and economic development, provide a structured framework for international collaboration.

This architecture matters because it moves beyond abstract commitments to AI ethics, outlining specific areas where developing nations face common obstacles and could benefit from coordinated action. Whether addressing the computational resource gap that constrains AI research in smaller economies or establishing safety protocols appropriate for diverse regulatory environments, these domains acknowledge that emerging markets require tailored solutions rather than technology transfer alone.

The emphasis on human capital development recognises that technological advancement without skilled workforces creates dependency rather than empowerment. Similarly, the focus on democratising AI resources tackles head-on the concentration of computational power that threatens to entrench existing global inequalities in the AI era.

India brings particular credibility to this conversation through its demonstrated capacity for large-scale digital implementation. The country's experience deploying digital public infrastructure, from biometric identification systems reaching over a billion citizens to unified payment interfaces processing millions of transactions daily, offers practical insights into equitable technology distribution.

This track record becomes especially relevant as developing nations confront a growing computational divide. Access to high-performance computing resources, essential for training sophisticated AI models, remains concentrated in wealthy nations and major technology corporations. New Delhi's proposal to address this asymmetry through shared infrastructure and collaborative research facilities represents a potentially significant shift in how AI capabilities might be distributed globally.

The infrastructure question extends beyond raw computing power to include datasets, algorithmic frameworks, and technical expertise, resources that determine whether nations can develop AI solutions tailored to their specific contexts or must rely on imported systems designed for different realities.

The summit's value proposition extends across different constituencies.

For developing nations, it provides a platform to collectively articulate technology governance priorities before international standards become entrenched. For multinational enterprises, it offers entry points into rapidly expanding markets characterised by unique challenges and opportunities, from multilingual natural language processing to AI applications in resource-constrained environments.

Development institutions and bilateral partners gain exposure to policy frameworks attempting to balance innovation encouragement with social protection, particularly relevant as AI's economic impacts intensify. For India itself, the gathering serves as a statement of technological maturity and policy leadership, positioning the nation as a convener capable of shaping rather than merely responding to global technology trajectories.

The convergence of these interests creates potential for substantive outcomes beyond ceremonial declarations, whether through joint research initiatives, shared computing facilities, or coordinated approaches to AI regulation that respect national sovereignty while enabling cross-border collaboration.

Perhaps most significantly, the summit represents an attempt to shift AI discourse beyond zero-sum competition toward collaborative problem-solving. While geopolitical tensions increasingly frame technology development as strategic rivalry, India's emphasis on inclusive growth and shared challenges offers an alternative framework-one particularly appealing to nations seeking to benefit from AI without becoming dependent on any single technology ecosystem.

The focus on trustworthy, secure systems alongside economic growth reflects hard-learned lessons about technology adoption in diverse societies.

Questions of algorithmic bias, data sovereignty, energy consumption, and workforce displacement carry different implications across contexts, requiring governance approaches that accommodate varied developmental stages and priorities.

By centering discussions around concrete challenges improving agricultural yields, expanding healthcare access, enhancing educational outcomes the summit grounds AI conversations in developmental imperatives rather than abstract technological capabilities. This reorientation may prove crucial in ensuring AI serves genuine societal needs rather than creating solutions in search of problems.

As the summit unfolds, its success will ultimately be measured not by diplomatic attendance or declaration language, but by whether it catalyzes genuine cooperation on AI development reflecting Global South priorities. Can shared infrastructure initiatives materialise? Will collaborative research networks emerge? Can alternative governance models gain international traction?

For India, the stakes extend beyond immediate outcomes. The nation seeks recognition as a pivotal force in technology's trajectory not through market size alone, but through intellectual leadership on questions of equity, sustainability, and human-centered design. Whether this vision resonates beyond New Delhi will shape both AI's evolution and the developing world's place within it.

The summit takes place at a moment when technological trajectories remain fluid enough for intervention, yet momentum toward concentration of AI capabilities accelerates daily. India's gambit is that collective action among emerging economies can still influence outcomes that the Global South can move from being shaped by artificial intelligence to actively shaping it.

India's AI summit must deliver more than dialogue, it must deliver direction

The countdown to India's forthcoming AI Summit has begun, but the real clock is not measuring time. It is measuring expectation. Not just national expectation, but global anticipation. Because when India convenes the world today, it is no longer to observe or adapt. It is to architect.

This summit cannot be another gathering of impressive speeches, overlapping panels, and aspirational declarations that fade into conference archives. It must be a turning point, one that establishes India not merely as a participant in the global AI discourse, but as a systems designer of the future itself. For that to happen, the summit must be unapologetically outcome-driven.

AI summits across the world have often excelled at framing the future but faltered in structuring it. They generate momentum but rarely institutionalise it. They produce language, not mechanisms. India has the opportunity, and responsibility, to change that pattern. An outcome-driven summit means that every deliberation must answer three non-negotiable questions:What will change because this conversation happened?Who will implement that change?By when will the world see the result?

Clarity must replace generality. Measurable frameworks must replace thematic overlaps. Instead of parallel discussions on ethics, governance, innovation, infrastructure, and inclusion, all valuable but often fragmented, the summit must weave these into integrated implementation pathways. This requires disciplined design.

Each thematic track should culminate in tangible deliverables: regulatory templates, interoperable technical standards, capacity-building frameworks, cross-border research protocols, finaning models for AI public goods, and structured partnerships. The summit's legacy must not be a communiqué alone, but a blueprint. The world does not need more dialogue about AI's potential. It needs architecture for AI's deployment, responsibly, equitably, and at scale.

This summit will bring together an extraordinary diversity of stakeholders: Governments, researchers, industry leaders, startups, civil society, development institutions, and multilateral organisations.

Such diversity is a strength, but only if it is orchestrated, not merely assembled. Without intentional design, diversity can produce conceptual congestion. Similar ideas circulate across panels, priorities blur, and consensus becomes performative rather than operational.

India must demonstrate that convening power is not simply about bringing voices together, it is about aligning them toward shared execution. This means structured thematic boundaries, clear role definition for each stakeholder group, and synthesis mechanisms that prevent duplication.

Deliberations should function like coordinated systems engineering, not parallel commentary. The summit must feel less like a conference, and more like a strategic design lab for humanity's technological future.

Perhaps the most important question is not what the summit discusses, but what identity it expresses. Global audiences must not leave with the impression that India is replicating existing AI governance models with local adaptation. They must recognise that India is offering a distinctive philosophical and operational framework, one shaped by its civilisational worldview, developmental experience, and technological pragmatism. This is where the summit's vision, anchored in the symbolic architecture of chakras and the guiding triad of People, Progress, and Planet, becomes transformative rather than ornamental. The chakra is not merely a cultural motif. It represents motion with balance. Power with responsibility. Expansion with alignment. It is a profound metaphor for AI itself, a force that must remain dynamic yet centred, transformative yet anchored in ethical equilibrium.

By structuring the summit around seven chakras: Human Capital, Inclusion for Social Empowerment, Safe and Trusted AI, Resilience, Innovation, and Efficiency, Science, Democratising AI Resources and AI for Economic Growth and Social Good; India is not invoking symbolism for aesthetic appeal. It is designing a governance architecture, one that treats technological development as an integrated system of human capability, institutional responsibility, economic dynamism, and societal wellbeing.

Each chakra functions as a stabilising force in the AI ecosystem. Together, they create a model of technological evolution that is balanced, regenerative, and future-ready. By organising the summit around People, Progress, and Planet, India signals a foundational proposition: technological advancement cannot be separated from human dignity, developmental equity, and ecological stability. This is not an imported framework. It is an indigenous systems philosophy, one that integrates economic growth, social welfare, and environmental stewardship as interdependent rather than competing objectives. If articulated clearly, this becomes India's intellectual signature on global AI governance. For decades, the global technology narrative placed India in the role of scale provider, talent contributor, or market adopter. That era is closing. This summit must communicate, unmistakably, that India now operates across the full strategic value chain of technological transformation:

India strategises: shaping governance principles, regulatory models, and global cooperation frameworks. India designs: building digital public infrastructure, interoperable platforms, and inclusive technological ecosystems. India innovates: advancing research, entrepreneurship, and applied solutions across sectors from healthcare and agriculture to education and climate resilience.

India disseminates: scaling solutions across the Global South and beyond, transforming innovation into shared global capability.

This fourfold identity must become the summit's central message. Not declared rhetorically, but demonstrated structurally, through partnerships launched, frameworks adopted, and mechanisms institutionalised.

The world should leave recognising that India is not reacting to the future of AI. It is engineering pathways toward it. Perhaps the most profound shift underway is psychological. For the first time in the technological age, large parts of the world, especially the Global South, are not merely observing innovation hubs in the West or East. They are looking toward India as a model of how scale, inclusion, and sovereignty can coexist in digital transformation. This summit must consciously embrace that aspirational dimension.

To be an aspiration is to carry responsibility. It means demonstrating that technological leadership can be democratic, development-oriented, and globally cooperative rather than extractive or exclusionary. India's voice must therefore be confident but constructive. Ambitious but accountable. Visionary but implementable. The message must be clear: the future is not being negotiated elsewhere. It is being co-created here.

A summit achieves real success not when delegates applaud its closing session, but when its ideas permeate global discourse afterward. The vision of People, Progress, and Planet, symbolised through the chakra, must travel beyond policy circles into academic frameworks, corporate strategy, international development agendas, and public imagination. It must become a reference model.

This requires intentional dissemination: publications, open frameworks, international collaborations, training networks, digital knowledge platforms, and continuous multilateral engag ment. The summit must be the beginning of a global narrative cycle, not a single event. India must ensure that what is conceptualised here becomes operational everywhere. History rarely announces turning points. It simply presents moments that later generations recognise as decisive. This summit is one such moment.

If designed with precision, executed with clarity, and followed with commitment, it can mark the transition from a fragmented global AI conversation to a structured global AI order, one shaped significantly by Indian thinking. The world is watching not just what India will say, but what India will build. When participants depart, they should not merely remember insightful discussions. They should carry frameworks, partnerships, and implementation mandates. They should leave with the unmistakable impression that India does not simply convene conversations about the future. India constructs the systems that make the future possible. The countdown has begun. Now the world will see what India delivers.

Dear Oscars, we're more than just a vibe

There's something deeply frustrating about watching Indian films dazzle global audiences, dominate festival circuits, make it to prestigious lineups across Cannes, Berlin, Toronto,

Sundance, and then fall flat at the Oscars.

It's not because we lack great cinema. Far from it. Some of the finest, most emotionally layered, visually stunning, and narratively powerful films are being made right here. But when the time comes to show up on the biggest award stage, we either don't make the cut or get token recognition for a song or a moment that barely scratches the surface of what Indian cinema truly is. NaatuNaatu winning was brilliant, yes, but that can't be the bar we keep celebrating. It feels like the world loves to cheer for our rhythm but not always for our soul.

Take Homebound, for example. A beautiful, deeply intimate film that had all the ingredients for global acclaim. And yet, it was ignored. Snubbed. Quietly pushed aside in the Oscar conversation. And the worst part? This isn't new. It's a pattern. The kind of international acknowledgment Indian cinema gets still seems limited to what fits a certain expectation, colour, chaos, celebration, maybe a bit of suffering. Anything that demands a more nuanced gaze? Too often, it's met with silence.

But the real question isn't just why this happens. The real question is: What are we doing wrong in how we position ourselves? Because make no mistake, it's not always about merit. The Oscars aren't just about good cinema. They're about visibility, perception, lobbying, timing, and sustained presence. The films that win aren't always the best; they're the best positioned. And we haven't cracked that code. Not yet. International film festivals and the Oscars operate on two completely different operating systems. Festivals are about curation. They're driven by programmers and juries who are actively looking for fresh voices, new grammar, untold stories. There's a hunger there to discover something authentic. That's why you'll often find Indian indie and regional films doing well in these spaces; they're raw, rooted, daring. But the Oscars? That's not discovery. That's campaigning. That's a full-blown industry with publicists, screenings, whispers in trade rooms, coverage in Variety and Deadline, strategic releases, and emotionally smart marketing. The Academy is a massive machine. And to enter it, you need more than just a good film. You need a roadmap.

What hurts even more is how India treats its Oscar strategy. One film. Once a year. That's it. A single submission carrying the weight of an entire country's cinematic expression. We've got thousands of films being made in over 20 languages every year, but when it comes to the Oscars, we're down to a single entry. That one film is expected to represent the full spectrum of Indian storytelling, from folklore to urban realism, from high-concept myth to kitchen-sink drama. It's unfair to the film and to the country.

Other nations don't do this. They create an ecosystem. Korea didn't win an Oscar out of nowhere with Parasite.

They'd been building towards it for years, establishing auteurs, creating curiosity, showing up in festival circuits, releasing films with global appeal. So when Parasite arrived, it didn't feel like an outsider; it felt inevitable. In contrast, Indian films often arrive like visitors, not residents. We don't stay long enough in the global imagination. We don't play the long game.

And yes, let's address the elephant in the room: bias. It exists. The West still sees Indian cinema through the lens of stereotype, musicals, poverty, family drama, exotic lands, and arranged marriages. There's a subconscious slot Indian stories are placed in, and when we show up with something that breaks the mould, a queer love story, a quiet meditation on grief, a gritty psychological drama, it doesn't always register. But bias isn't the only villain here. Sometimes, we just don't make ourselves legible to the system. We expect recognition without fully entering the conversation.

This is where our own festivals come in. Indian film festivals need to stop being only about glitter and gala screenings. They should act as springboards for international positioning. We need to use IFFI, MAMI, and others as launchpads, not just to show off what we've made, but to build global strategies. Connect our filmmakers to international programmers, give them access to festival publicists, and train them in the art of building a global presence. The real job of a festival isn't just to celebrate cinema, it's to carry it forward into the world.

We also need to stop relying only on official channels for global placement. One government submission can't carry the weight. Instead, multiple films can and should be campaigned independently across different Oscar categories, Best International Feature, yes, but also Documentary, Animation, Screenplay, and even Short Film. Let's flood the space with our talent. Let's stop asking permission and start taking up space. The National Film Award juries may rethink their approach to the canvas of global cinema in the light of movies competing in the feature and non-feature categories.

At the heart of it all, we need a mindset shift. We have already arrived as a cinematic powerhouse. We don't need to prove we belong; we do. What we need now is a strategy. Continuity. And self-belief. We need to invest in storytelling, but also in story-framing. We need to believe that our cinema, whether it's a Tamil neo-noir, a Marathi courtroom drama, a Khasi-language coming-of-age story, or a Kashmiri political thriller, deserves to be on the world stage, not as an anomaly, but as a regular, recurring voice.

We're no longer the exotic outsider knocking on the gates. We are the culture that shaped global music, global cuisine, global fashion, and yes, global cinema too. The Oscars will catch up. But first, we have to show up like we belong. Not for a song. Not for a season. But for the long haul.

Quiet revolution: How traditional communication won the India-EU trade deal

At a time when diplomacy is increasingly performed in public, compressed into soundbites, hashtags and instant reactions, the India-EU Free Trade Agreement feels almost countercultural. After more than a decade of stalled negotiations and repeated false starts, one of the world's most consequential trade deals did not come together through urgency, pressure or dramatic breakthroughs. It came together quietly. That quiet matters. The India-EU FTA covers economies that together account for nearly a quarter of global GDP and close to 30 per cent of global trade. Its scale alone makes it historic. But what is more instructive than the numbers is how the deal was arrived at, and how it was communicated. This was not a negotiation driven by spectacle. It was shaped by patience, restraint and a deliberate return to traditional diplomatic communication.

In many ways, this agreement is less about tariffs and market access and more about trust. And trust, especially between complex partners with long memories of failed negotiations, does not emerge from performative diplomacy. It is built slowly, often away from the spotlight. This is also why the public framing of the agreement as "the mother of all deals" has been so effective. The phrase is bold but non-technical. It conveys scale without dragging the audience into the weeds of sectoral carve-outs or tariff schedules. As a piece of political communication, it works because it anchors perception early. It tells people this is historic before the details can fracture the narrative. In a crowded media environment, that kind of framing is not accidental; it is strategic.

What made the India-EU FTA possible was not a single moment of convergence, but a sustained process of communication that unfolded over time. The first, and perhaps most important, shift was the decision to reset the tone of engagement altogether. After years in which trade talks had become synonymous with deadlock, both sides consciously avoided reopening old grievances or assigning blame. That choice was neither naïve nor evasive. It was a recognition that progress required a clean slate, not a post-mortem.

The success of the India-EU FTA can best be understood through the classical framework of the 5Ds of diplomacy: Dialogue, Discussion, Decision, Delivery and Dissemination. Far from abstract theory, these five dimensions shaped how the agreement was communicated into existence. Dialogue rebuilt trust through sustained engagement without reopening old grievances; Discussion prioritised listening over positioning, allowing differences to be acknowledged without derailing progress; Decision was signalled through calm political resolve rather than triumphalist rhetoric; Delivery focused on communicating balance, preparedness and safeguards, not just outcomes; Dissemination ensured legitimacy by tailoring messages across stakeholders, from businesses to farmers to young professionals.

Dialogue resumed across levels - leaders, ministers, negotiators and technical experts - and it did so without the pressure of immediate deliverables. Conversations were framed around long-term alignment rather than transactional wins: supply-chain resilience, sustainability transitions, talent mobility and economic security. Even when disagreements remained unresolved, engagement did not stop. That continuity itself sent a message of seriousness. In traditional diplomacy, showing up consistently is communication.

In a media culture that often treats silence as stagnation, the India-EU process revealed the opposite. The absence of public drama often signals that the real work is actually happening.

Equally important was the way discussions were conducted. Previous rounds of negotiations had collapsed under the weight of hardened positions, with each side asserting demands while talking past the other. This time, listening became central. Sensitive issues — agriculture, sustainability standards, regulatory alignment and data governance —were not forced into artificial resolution. They were acknowledged, contextualised and, in some cases, deliberately sequenced over time.

This shift in approach produced tangible results. The agreement secured preferential access to European markets across 97 per cent of tariff lines, covering almost all of India's export value, while preserving policy space for sensitive sectors such as dairy and cereals. Such outcomes rarely come from aggressive negotiation; they emerge when communication allows calibration rather than confrontation.

Political leadership mattered, but so did its tone. Messaging throughout remained measured and forward-looking, with no triumphalism or talk of winners and losers. By presenting the agreement as strategic alignment rather than concession, leaders stabilised expectations, reduced domestic pressure on negotiators, and strengthened confidence among markets and stakeholders.

Delivery, too, was handled as a communication exercise rather than a mere procedural step. The way the agreement was explained mattered as much as the agreement itself. Safeguards were clearly articulated. Phased tariff liberalisation was framed not as disruption, but as preparation. MSME-friendly compliance pathways and sector-specific opportunities were highlighted in terms of employment and competitiveness. Labour-intensive sectors such as textiles, leather, and gems and jewellery were positioned as early beneficiaries, reinforcing the idea that the deal was balanced rather than abrupt.

Dissemination was equally deliberate. There was no single, generic narrative pushed across audiences. Businesses were reassured about predictability and integration into European value chains.

Professionals and students were informed about expanded mobility opportunities across services sectors. Farmers and traditional industries were addressed through explicit safeguards and selective access. This tailoring mattered. It turned the FTA from a diplomatic milestone into something that different constituencies could recognise as relevant to them.

Soft power quietly reinforced this process. Symbolic gestures, cultural sensitivity, personal connections and visible respect added emotional credibility to institutional negotiations. These moments did not dominate headlines, but they deepened trust. They reminded stakeholders that this was not just a commercial transaction, but a relationship grounded in mutual recognition and mutual restraint. The broader geopolitical context also shaped how the deal was communicated. At a time when the global trading system feels increasingly fragile, with traditional guarantors of stability stepping back,

India and the EU were careful not to frame the FTA as opportunistic or reactive. Instead, it was positioned as an exercise in predictability and shared responsibility. Differences - whether regulatory or geopolitical - were acknowledged rather than denied, and deferred rather than dramatised. That realism made convergence possible where perfection would have ensured failure.

Ultimately, the India-EU FTA is a reminder of something diplomacy has always known but often forgets: communication is not an accessory to negotiation; it is the negotiation. By privileging dialogue over drama, listening over posturing, symbolism over spectacle and patience over publicity, India and the EU delivered a deal that once seemed unattainable.

In a fractured global environment obsessed with immediacy, the success of the India-EU FTA offers a quieter lesson. Enduring partnerships are not built through viral moments or rhetorical excess. They are built through sustained engagement, disciplined messaging and the confidence to let substance mature away from the noise, until it is strong enough to speak for itself.

AI Impact Summit: Igniting India's 'JanAI' for Viksit Bharat

New Delhi is set to host the AI Impact Summit 2026, a landmark event poised to redefine India's trajectory in artificial intelligence. Scheduled as a beacon of innovation, this summit transcends traditional conferences; it's a clarion call for India's emergence as a world leader in AI development. In an era where AI shapes economies, societies and geopolitics, the summit positions India not as a follower, but as a trailblazer. By fusing cutting-edge technology with grassroots participation, it embodies the spirit of transforming AI into a "people's movement" — AI for larger impact or 'JanAI' - propelling the nation towards Viksit Bharat, a developed India by 2047.

At its core, the summit addresses a pressing need: a robust communication strategy that elevates it from an elite gathering to a national phenomenon. Mere announcements won't suffice; India must craft a narrative that resonates with every citizen, turning the event into a household conversation. Building a "people's connect" demands innovative outreach — social media campaigns, regional town halls, and AI-powered apps that let citizens co-create summit agendas. By scaling participation, the summit fosters Jan Bhagidari (public involvement) and ignites a Jan Aandolan (people's movement), much like successful national drives such as Swachh Bharat or Digital India. Crucially, this approach also recognises that trust in emerging technologies is built through clarity, consistency and transparency. Communicating not just the promise of AI but also its risks, safeguards and accountability mechanisms helps create informed confidence among citizens. Translating complex ideas on AI governance, ethics and safety into accessible, multilingual narratives ensures broader understanding without oversimplification. Meaningful two-way communication, where feedback is invited, acknowledged and reflected, strengthens legitimacy and public ownership, ensuring that AI governance in India is not merely designed for the people, but shaped with them.

Strategically, the AI Impact Summit stands as one of India's most critical events on the global stage. As superpowers race for AI supremacy, India's demographic dividend, with over 1.4 billion people and a burgeoning tech talent pool, offers unmatched potential. Hosting the summit in the heart of the capital signals Delhi's readiness to lead. It will convene global CEOs, policymakers, ethicists and innovators to deliberate on AI governance, ethical deployment and inclusive growth. For India, this isn't just prestige; it's a pivot towards self-reliance (Atmanirbhar Bharat).

The event underscores how technology can accelerate India's journey towards Viksit Bharat, the goal of becoming a developed nation by 2047. AI, when deployed inclusively, is projected to contribute trillions of dollars to economic growth, and India aims to ensure these gains reach the last mile.

A defining strength of the summit lies in how it is communicated to the nation. Rather than remaining confined to elite policy rooms, the India-AI Impact Summit is designed to become a household conversation. Drawing on the spirit of Jan Bhagidari and Jan Aandolan, its outreach strategy seeks to demystify AI and anchor it in everyday life. A coordinated media presence, regional radio, podcasts and digital platforms - from Instagram Reels to short-form videos - will ensure the summit resonates equally in metropolitan centres and rural heartlands, positioning ethical and inclusive AI as India's defining contribution to the world.

At its philosophical core, the summit is guided by three foundational Sutras - People, Planet and Progress — which blend civilisational values with modern governance. These principles shape India's vision of multilateral AI cooperation. The focus on People ensures that human dignity, equity and empowerment remain central. Planet anchors AI innovation in sustainability and climate resilience. Progress commits to ensuring that AI-driven advancements in healthcare, education, agriculture and public services are accessible and fair. Together, these Sutras provide direction for global discussions, steering them towards shared prosperity rather than narrow technological dominance.

Translating these principles into action are seven interconnected Chakras that structure the summit's agenda and partnerships. Human capital development focuses on skilling and workforce augmentation, with nationwide hackathons, youth-led challenges and influencer-driven engagement mobilising students and young professionals at scale. Social inclusion and empowerment address algorithmic bias, accessibility and multilingual AI, brought alive through human stories shared via regional media and podcasts that highlight technology's impact on marginalised communities. The emphasis on safe and trusted AI builds public confidence through transparent governance discussions, animated explainers and widely shared leadership messages that turn ethics into a subject of everyday conversation.

Resilience, innovation and efficiency are advanced through a push for lean and sustainable AI solutions, demonstrated via real-world use cases aligned with national initiatives such as Swachh Bharat. Scientific collaboration is strengthened through Global South partnerships, positioning India as a hub for frontier research through broadcasts, documentaries and digital discourse led by scientists. Democratising AI resources — data, compute and models — encourages open participation, supported by digital platforms that invite public input and foster a sense of collective ownership. Finally, AI for economic growth and social good highlights public-sector applications and cross-border initiatives, amplified through success stories from farmers, visual economic insights and high-visibility endorsements that make AI aspirational and relatable.

The legacy of the India-AI Impact Summit 2026 extends far beyond its two-day schedule. It lays the foundation for recurring global engagements, pan-India AI corridors and durable international frameworks. By championing JanAI - ethical, inclusive and powered by public participation, India offers the world, particularly the Global South, an alternative model of AI leadership. Supported by institutional collaboration and growing international interest, the summit advances the trinity of innovation, equity and sustainability that defines Viksit Bharat. In doing so, New Delhi will not merely host a global event; it will help redefine the future of artificial intelligence, demonstrating how technology can deliver shared prosperity from the grassroots to the global stage. Equally significant is the summit's contribution to strengthening trust in AI governance. By emphasising transparency, public understanding and continuous dialogue, it reinforces the idea that effective AI frameworks succeed only when they are widely understood and responsibly implemented. The summit also sets a precedent for treating accountability and learning as core features of innovation, normalising open discussion on risks, safeguards and course correction. Over time, this approach can deepen institutional credibility, encourage voluntary compliance and inspire global cooperation rooted in shared values rather than technological dominance alone. As India moves towards its 2047 vision, the AI Impact Summit 2026 stands as a marker of how leadership in the digital age is defined not just by technological capability, but by the ability to build confidence, inclusion and collective ownership in shaping the future.

Streaming in flux: Why 2026 will redefine the OTT playbook

In the day and age of content creation, virality, and disruption, apprehensions do remain regarding the trajectory and growth of the OTT space in 2026. Analysts are already debating whether the fight for space, attention, and consistency will usher in a new era of content experimentation, digital disruption, and new forms of storytelling in the OTT space in the months to follow.

As globalisation is reinforced through collaboration and partnership, the roots of a global entertainment landscape are bound to reflect the contours and complexion of a vibrant creator's economy. As a consequence, the terrain of the OTT ecosystem will be a reckoning force in outlining the content, outreach, and the building blocks for the parameters that will define and design the contours of a creator's economy in 2026. Due to the dynamics and instinctive push of OTT platforms, it has triggered and catalysed the positioning and onboarding of new ideas, templates, voices, techniques, and tools woven and embedded in technology. The OTT profile in 2026 will be scanned on a 24x7 basis by analysts and commentators to review consumption, content, collaboration, and consistency in the ecosystem and the changes therein.

One of the emerging challenges in 2026 will be the forms and formats of storytelling in order to connect and engage with diverse audiences, perspectives, and narratives within the given OTT canvas. A key determinant of the success rate will be the emerging technological and content architecture. How far have the diverse platforms been able to optimise business models, break the silence of cross-sectoral bottlenecks and access, and outline a new growth path shaped by bold ideas, courage, and connection in thought and audience appeal? Storytelling in the OTT space is bound to be influenced by the buzz of smartphone penetration and data disaggregation, leading to new forms of authenticity, mindsets, audience needs, and instant real-time audience engagement. Content design and management will need to address the challenges of cross-cultural synchronisation, wherein ideas, themes, and languages correlate, coexist, and collate for better visibility, appreciation, and impact. The swipe of a smartphone, press of a button, and self-belief have led the consumer to become a passionate curator of creative thinking, ideation, and hyper-curiosity, designing instant information flow on a 24x7 basis.

Business modelling will be a huge OTT challenge due to the demand-and-supply equation. The profitability index will be a key determinant in view of over-optimised content flow, erratic buyer-seller equations, multiple business model experimentation, and the tug of war between cost, profit, and sustainability options. "Consumer is king," the often-quoted tagline, also adds to the stress and pulls for major OTT players. It will be a herculean task managing audience aspirations, pricing and subscription models, and the weariness accompanying content fatigue due to a lack of original content.

2026 will truly be a daunting task for OTT players in view of content weariness, saturation, the need for cultural and thematic integration, the search for hybrid revenue modelling, high production costs, and the need for redesigning content formats through new topics, sequels, and creative expressions.

A key feature in the OTT 2026 growth curve will be the perfect amalgamation between creativity, technology, planners, and data managers. The OTT landscape will witness a blend of storytelling woven with data analytics, giving it an emotional interactive push, preparing the ground for an innovation index that is monetised with new vigour and without friction, and a year of premium content for audiences, multi-device compatibility, and hybrid modelling for audiences to exercise options.

For India, in 2026, the OTT growth story will be determined by the diversity and complexity of our ecosystem. The touchpoints relate to languages, dialects, culture, home-grown realities, and the thematic and narrative interface.

In order to be in a win-win situation, the battle and tussle of narratives will occupy centre stage, with protagonist-driven narratives adding new spice and flavour.

One should not be surprised to witness a new face, phenomenon, or wave of storytelling in unpredictable, creative, and innovative ways. 2026 in India may witness a fine balance between contemporary themes, cultural legacy and myths, and innovative thinking. This will reinforce the OTT bandwidth to operate with a conscience that does not merely play to the gallery or algorithm-driven programming. The year may also face challenges related to new ideas on gender, identity, the deep consequences of misinformation, and the emerging pitfalls of binge-watching. For OTT platforms, 2026 provides an opportunity to mirror expectations and aspirations, portraying life and narratives from the fringes of human existence and society, giving voice and space to bold ideas, styles, and generational thoughts. This is bound to capture India's

social reality through screens and streaming devices.

A game-changer in 2026 will be the virality associated with word of mouth for OTT viewing. This is surely a new form of content acceptance and audience viewing. Audiences today in the OTT ecosystem tend to be loyal to words, themes, and innovative thought processes rather than genres and brands. As a consequence, there is a "cultural renaissance" to watch content across different shows and formats. Hence, language shifts will surely continue to be a game-changer and buzz. India in 2026, in the OTT space, will explore contexts beyond genres and languages, diluting boundaries and leading to new viewership bases, accessibility, and an unspoken, undefined diversity that is simple yet complex. The language lens has certainly become blurred, hence the need to understand content through "wide-angle" spectacles and new verticals of curiosity. We are perhaps entering a new age of the D's in the OTT space-distortion, disruption, dissemination, diversification, and dedication.

2026 will also be a critical signpost for the OTT space to integrate innovation with commerce, cultural learning, and storytelling through contemporary issues and audience-preferred protagonists. This will be the year for strengthening the reach of linguistic diversity in the viewing space. The challenge for platforms will be to balance continuity, change, reality, and societal commentary through a crisp and nuanced interface and screen engagement.

Beyond virality: Reclaiming credibility in the communication matrix of 2026

The communication matrix in 2026 is bound to undergo a strategic shift. A shift that reflects complex geopolitical scenarios, varied outreach tools, differentiated content design, and the sheer plurality of issues competing for attention. Issues related to ideas, perceptions, identity, and power, and the diverse communication stakeholders defining the path of the information gateway.

The communication ecosystem, year after year, defies established principles of interaction at the individual, national, and global levels. What was once linear, hierarchical, and relatively stable has now become circular, fragmented, and fluid. We may call it an 'information flux', a constant state of churn, leading to a rethink and reconfiguration of what constitutes ideal dissemination, reception, and interpretation of information.

This flux is not accidental. It is shaped by the collapse of traditional information monopolies, the rise of decentralised platforms, and the democratisation of content creation. Authority is no longer inherited; it is contested, negotiated, and often algorithmically assigned. In such an environment, communication is no longer just about transmission, but about contestation of meaning, credibility, and intent.

In 2026, the matrix will be overtly influenced by the malaise of instant communication, diffused attention spans, and the profound impact of technology woven through artificial intelligence and algorithmically induced communication. Speed has become both an asset and a liability. The moot question and the central challenge in 2026 will be the need to balance consistency and clarity in communication vis-à-vis the monstrosity of information overload and deepening communication polarisation between the real, unreal, virtual, and fake. Truth itself is no longer singular; it exists in competing versions shaped by belief systems, echo chambers, and selective exposure.

This fragmentation places immense pressure on communicators to anchor narratives without appearing rigid, outdated, or dismissive. Policymakers, in particular, will need to be wary of the impulse to beat the finishing line merely to create an immediate visible impact. The race for immediacy often comes at the cost of accuracy, nuance, and long-term trust. Practitioners, therefore, will need to design an ecosystem that reinforces dialogue, interconnectivity, outreach, and sustained information flow, while consciously warding off the perils of disinformation, misinformation, and narrative fatigue. Communication in 2026 will demand patience in an impatient world.

‘Credibility’ will be the core challenge for communication practitioners in the new year. Traditional modes and models of communication have been brushed aside by new tools, ideas, and themes dominating the narrative space. Institutional authority, once taken for granted, is now questioned, scrutinised, and frequently undermined. There is an urgent need to reposition communication, trust, and authenticity through multiple modes and mechanisms that go beyond optics. In 2026, credibility cannot be built or sustained purely through AI- and algorithm-driven, agenda-oriented narratives or through technology-heavy processes that privilege volume over value.

The pitfalls of information abundance are already visible: over-starched outreach strategies, performative storytelling, and messaging that prioritises virality over veracity. Credibility must instead emerge from coherence: a strong interconnect between message, medium, method, and process across platforms. Without this alignment, even the most sophisticated communication strategies risk appearing hollow. In the new matrix, trust will not be declared; it will have to be earned repeatedly.

A robust mechanism will need to be strategically placed and continuously refined to tackle the menace of virality-driven disinformation and unfiltered messaging. The growing credibility gap cannot be bridged through reactive firefighting alone. It will require proactive engagement, strengthened media literacy processes, concrete accountability frameworks, and transparent feedback loops. Narrative supervision will become as important as narrative creation. This is especially critical in a landscape where content tools and communication methods are increasingly weaponised, used to influence public opinion, destabilise societies, and crumble democratic discourse.

Perhaps one of the most concerning developments within this ecosystem has been the rapid decline of interpersonal communication between stakeholders due to relentless technological bombardment. Screens have replaced conversations, metrics have replaced listening, and immediacy has replaced empathy. As a consequence, the importance of personal connection in the communication terrain has faded, pushing one of the most effective traditional tools of trust-building to the margins. In a hyper-digital environment, the absence of human reassurance amplifies distrust, emotional fatigue, and disengagement.

Narrative building through different formats and tools has also undergone fundamental change, driven by 24×7 information machines and real-time analytics. Data now outlines storytelling, often brushing aside traditional methods of content collation, evaluation, and contextualisation. While dissemination has become decentralised and instant, storytelling itself has become fragile and complex. Messages are no longer consumed in entirety; they are skimmed, clipped, repurposed, and reinterpreted.

The immediate need, therefore, is to outline a communication architecture that captures not just information, but mood, flavour, emotion, and intent. Communication today is as much about feeling as it is about fact. Modelling of information has become more complex due to the expanding role of non-state actors and tools that often defy human touch, rationality, and ethical restraint. Unfortunately, the dynamics of the pen-and-paper interface, reflection, pause, and deliberation, have been lost in the haze of push-button communication.

The communication architecture in 2026 cannot afford to negate the 'human element.' Technology may enhance reach, but it cannot replace judgment, empathy, or moral responsibility. The key inputs for this model must remain adaptation and adaptability, of interface, interaction, and exchange, without surrendering the core values of communication.

2026, therefore, demands a 'hybrid model' of communication, where media literacy education becomes a central pillar rather than a peripheral concern. In the age of information splurge, it is critical that individuals, societies, nations, and the global order develop the capacity to evaluate sources, intent, and credibility within the information landscape. Media literacy is no longer optional; it is foundational.

Ethical imprints within the communication system must be reconfigured to reflect this new reality. The hybrid model should foster a stronger connection between information, connectivity, clarity, and technical innovation. Such an approach may lead to the gradual restoration of institutional credibility that has steadily eroded over the past decade. The emerging communication dividend must reinforce the old saying, "A picture speaks a thousand words. Seeing is believing."

Yet, visuals too must be contextualised, for images without integrity can mislead as easily as words. In the hybrid configuration, 2026 will truly leave its imprint if the communication matrix fine-tunes templates that acknowledge, rather than dismiss, the emotional dimension associated with news, views, presentation, and disinformation. Emotion cannot be eliminated from communication; it must be understood and responsibly engaged.

Communication in 2026 will require 'speed limits' on the information highway, limits that deter fake news, trust erosion, clouded perceptions, narrative insensitivity, and the growing lack of empathy. The obsession with speed and scale must give way to relevance and responsibility. Without such recalibration, communication risks becoming louder but not wiser, faster but not truer, expansive yet increasingly disconnected from reality. Ultimately, the success of the communication matrix in 2026 will lie not in how much is said, but in how meaningfully it is understood.

Translating trust into action: Communication is central to AI governance

Governance frameworks fail not because they are poorly designed but because they are poorly understood. Well-intentioned policies, regulatory guidance, and institutional architectures become meaningless if the people who must implement them — and the publics they serve — do not understand what they mean, why they matter, and how they will improve outcomes.

This is the communication imperative at the heart of modern AI governance. As societies grapple with how to harness artificial intelligence's potential while mitigating its risks, clear, strategic, and transparent communication emerges not as a supplementary function but as foundational to governance itself.

Trust is the bedrock of any governance system, yet it is also the most fragile. Without trust, policies fail. Adoption stagnates. Compliance weakens. Citizens disengage. Trust is not created by issuing regulations or publishing policy documents — it is built through consistent, transparent, and honest communication. Trust architecture requires communication at multiple levels simultaneously. Institutions must explain their decisions transparently, acknowledge uncertainties and risks honestly, and demonstrate accountability when problems emerge. When communicators consistently say what institutions will do and then follow through, trust accumulates. When there are gaps between promises and reality, trust evaporates rapidly.

In AI governance specifically, the communication challenge is acute. The technology is complex and evolving rapidly. Public understanding varies widely. Media narratives oscillate between utopian enthusiasm and catastrophic fear. Communicators must build nuanced understanding — acknowledging genuine opportunities and legitimate risks - in a media landscape that often rewards extreme positions.

The most effective governance communication establishes "informed confidence" - where stakeholders understand the challenges, trust that competent institutions are managing them, and believe they have voice and agency in how governance unfolds.

Policy communication faces a central challenge: translating complex concepts into comprehensible language without sacrificing accuracy. Modern AI governance addresses intricate topics — graded liability systems, data-protection exemptions, classification of actor roles, incident-reporting mechanisms, algorithmic-fairness assessment, and deepfake-detection standards. These technical and legal matters must be understandable to vastly different audiences: policymakers in state governments, compliance officers in start-ups, risk managers in financial institutions, civil-society organisations, and informed citizens. Each requires different communication approaches.

Communicators face a genuine tension: translating without oversimplifying, making content accessible without losing technical accuracy. This requires deliberate design choices - using plain language, providing concrete examples, employing visual explanations, tailoring messages for different audiences, and ensuring multilingual availability. This design-centric approach recognises that understandability is foundational. When policymakers understand regulatory rationale, they implement more effectively. When industry understands liability implications, it makes more responsible decisions. When civil society grasps accountability mechanisms, it can hold institutions to account.

Governance frameworks are stronger when they incorporate diverse perspectives, stakeholders feel heard, and decisions are transparently explained. Communicators orchestrate this engagement by designing meaningful consultation processes, establishing accessible feedback mechanisms, and demonstrating how inputs shaped decisions.

Multi-stakeholder engagement serves multiple functions simultaneously. It identifies implementation challenges early. It builds constituencies invested in policy success. It ensures marginalised voices are part of the conversation from the start. It enhances decision legitimacy, increasing voluntary compliance.

In diverse societies, meaningful engagement requires particular care. Participation cannot be limited to policy elites. It must actively reach excluded communities using local languages, community forums, mobile platforms, and trusted local organisations.

What creates accountability? One key mechanism is transparency — when organisations publicly explain decisions, compliance efforts, and what happens when things go wrong. Yet transparency alone is insufficient; accountability emerges when transparency is expected, public-scrutiny mechanisms exist, and institutions demonstrate learning from failures.

Incident reporting presents a significant communication challenge. Conventionally, organisations hide failures, fearing reputational damage. Emerging governance approaches recommend a different model:

normalising incident reporting, perceiving it as responsible rather than negligent, and treating incidents as learning opportunities.

This cultural shift is fundamentally a communication challenge. Communicators must reframe how failure is understood — showing that reporting problems signals competence and responsibility. This requires sustained communication where regulators publicly analyse incident patterns and organisations explain what they learned. Governance increasingly relies on voluntary measures — industry codes, certifications, and standards — as regulation complements them. Yet voluntary compliance succeeds only when frameworks are visible, understood, and valued. Communicators build narratives around voluntary compliance. They make certification programmes credible and meaningful. They provide recognition for responsible practices through media coverage and investor communications.

They create visible markers — certifications, ratings, endorsements — that consumers and investors recognise and reward. This narrative-building work is essential because voluntary frameworks lack enforcement mechanisms. Compliance depends on reputation and stakeholder perception. Well-communicated frameworks become meaningful; poorly communicated ones remain marginal.

As societies implement governance frameworks addressing complex challenges, communication effectiveness determines success. Well-designed policies fail if not understood. Regulations face resistance if not explained. Accountability mechanisms fail if not transparent. Communicators are essential architects of effective governance. They build trust enabling adoption. They translate complexity into accessibility. They facilitate multi-stakeholder dialogue. They create accountability through transparency. They ensure policy reaches and protects all communities. In this sense, communication is not something added after governance is designed — it is foundational to governance itself. It is how principles become practice, how regulations achieve compliance, how institutions build legitimacy.

The most effective governance will not be determined solely by policy sophistication. It will be determined by how well those frameworks are understood, believed in, and embraced by the institutions and people responsible for their success.

Branding works because humans are, fundamentally, storytellers

The recent launch of When Branding Met the Movies at the World Book Fair in Delhi became a wide-ranging conversation on how cinema, culture and commerce intersect. Written by Chaitanya K. Prasad along with Zoya Ahmad and Vaishnavie Srinivasan, the book examines branding and how audiences connect with films long before the first frame appears.

Drawing from Indian and global cinema, the session explored how actors and filmmakers themselves function as brands, why audiences buy into stories as much as stars, and how films today must balance cultural authenticity with global reach.

'Branding is the art of making people feel something about your product, service, or in our case, a movie'

During the session, multiple dimensions of branding were unpacked, beginning with the idea that actors themselves function as brands -and in some cases, directors like James Cameron and Christopher Nolan are brands in their own right, shaping audience expectations even before a film is released.

"Branding is the art of making people feel something about your product, service, or in our case, a movie, before they've even experienced it," said Chaitanya K. Prasad, a retired senior civil servant who currently serves as Head of Promotion and Outreach at the Ministry of Education, Government of India.

He added,"It's like being a master chef - but instead of mixing flavours, you're combining emotions, visuals, sounds and experiences to create something that sticks in people's minds, like a song you hear once and can't stop humming.

At its core, branding is about giving something—anything - a distinct personality that people can recognise, remember and hopefully fall in love with."

He explained that branding works because humans are, fundamentally, storytellers. Audiences don't simply buy tickets or products; they buy into narratives about who they are and what they value. In cinema, this instinct is amplified because films themselves are built out of stories.

"When you choose a Christopher Nolan film, you're choosing to be someone who appreciates complex cinema," he said. "When you buy a Marvel ticket, you're joining a community of fans."

'How do you speak to everyone while still honouring where the story comes from?'

Tracing how branding evolved alongside cinema, he noted that contemporary film marketing has grown increasingly sophisticated. "Branding has gone full 3D chess lately," he remarked, pointing to how films are now positioned simultaneously across platforms, geographies and audience segments.

Turning to global examples, he highlighted how branding enables films to travel across cultures without losing their roots. "The film world is more connected than ever. Movies now release across countries and languages at the same time," he said. "But that creates a challenge - how do you speak to everyone while still honouring where the story comes from?"

Parasite (2019), directed by Bong Joon-ho, offered a model solution. Though deeply rooted in South Korean class politics, its branding foregrounded universal themes, genre fluidity and bold storytelling. Audiences across the world found points of identification without the film sacrificing its cultural specificity. Its Oscar win, Prasad argued, was not just a triumph for one film, but a milestone for global cinema, proving that authenticity need not be diluted for international success.

He cited RRR as another example of culturally grounded global branding. SS Rajamouli's historical epic leaned unapologetically into spectacle—larger-than-life heroes, heightened emotion and gravity-defying action—while Oscar recognition and streaming visibility carried it far beyond audiences unfamiliar with Telugu cinema. Similarly, The White Tiger (2021), adapted from Aravind Adiga's Booker Prize-winning novel, used branding to frame its sharp socio-political critique in a way that resonated internationally, without softening its Indian context.

As films increasingly cross borders, Prasad concluded, branding must walk a careful line - balancing the global with the local, scale with specificity, and reach with rootedness. In today's cinema ecosystem, he suggested, the films that endure are not those that flatten their identities, but those that know exactly who they are.

The Age of Influence: Reimagining Communication as Strategic Power

In an era defined by information overload, narrative warfare, and the relentless churn of digital media, understanding how influence is constructed and wielded has become crucial for nations, institutions, and individuals alike. My recent book '*The Age of Influence: Thoughts on Communication in Geopolitics, Soft Power and Branding*' arrives at a moment when the architecture of communication itself is undergoing profound transformation, offering not answers but essential questions about how we shape and are shaped by narratives in the modern world.

The analysis of the theme traces the evolving contours of the contemporary communication landscape. Diverse themes ranging from geostrategic communication and soft power to cinema, artificial intelligence, branding, and film festivals, it positions communication not as a peripheral concern but as central to how power is exercised and contested in the 21st century.

Three interconnected insights define the influence paradigm that impinges on different themes and ecosystems globally. First, the power of influence lies fundamentally in storytelling and narrative building. Whether in policy, commerce, culture, or diplomacy, those who can craft compelling narratives wield disproportionate influence over outcomes and perceptions.

Second, in times of conflict, whether military, economic, or ideological, it is not merely whose army or economy prevails but whose narrative wins. This has profound implications for how nations approach both hard and soft power in an age where perception often matters as much as material capability.

Third, technological capabilities must be matched by ethical frameworks and governance structures. The democratization of powerful communication tools like AI represents progress only if accompanied by safeguards against their weaponization for malicious purposes.

Taking into account key issues related to the central argument supports the case for a new world information order, arguments especially pertinent as nations across the Global South assert their voices on global platforms. The need for narrative sovereignty has gained urgency in a world where questions of who tells the story, whose voice dominates, and how information ecosystems are structured have become critical to ensuring equity and authenticity in global discourse.

Communication is not viewed merely as a channel of dissemination but as a powerful site of negotiation and identity formation. In a world increasingly shaped by narrative warfare and symbolic politics, the ability to craft, read, and reshape stories has become a critical skill for nations seeking to define themselves rather than be defined by others.

This framing challenges the traditional hierarchies of global media and information flows. It asks uncomfortable questions about whose perspectives dominate international discourse, which narratives gain traction and why, and how developing nations can assert agency in shaping their own stories. These are not abstract academic concerns but practical questions of power, perception, and sovereignty in an interconnected world.

A dominant idea that should be discussed in the whole influence architecture is the role of cinema and celebrity culture in shaping collective consciousness. The rise of film festivals as global cultural forums, the strategic branding of public figures, and the evolving relationship between entertainment and nation-building are examined not as peripheral cultural phenomena but as central to how nations articulate soft power and how societies understand themselves.

It is important to note that the analysis pays particular attention to how Indian cinema has emerged as a cultural export, influencing perceptions and creating bridges across borders. The role of storytelling in diplomacy, the aesthetic choices that carry political weight, and the global appetite for regional narratives are analyzed not as cultural curiosities but as strategic tools of engagement with tangible geopolitical implications.

This perspective represents a significant departure from traditional conceptions of power that privilege military might and economic leverage. Soft power, the ability to attract and persuade rather than coerce, operates through cultural channels that are often underestimated by policymakers schooled in conventional statecraft. Cinema, with its emotional resonance and narrative power, represents one of the most potent instruments of soft power available to nations.

There is a deep dive in geostrategic communication today to understand The Double-Edged Sword of Technology. The analysis also grapples with the rampant usage of artificial intelligence in contemporary communication, particularly its role in spreading misinformation and disinformation. This presents one of the defining tensions of our age: while AI tools must be democratized to ensure broader access and innovation, their democratization risks enabling weaponization by malicious actors.

The challenge lies in navigating this paradox. Concentration of powerful communication technologies in the hands of a few raises concerns about monopolistic control and digital colonialism. Yet widespread distribution of the same tools creates vulnerabilities to coordinated disinformation campaigns, deepfakes, and algorithmically amplified falsehoods that can destabilize democracies and undermine public trust.

Providing solutions to this dilemma is not easy, but a moot question is framed for the policymakers, technologists, and citizens must collectively address. In doing so, it positions AI not merely as a technical challenge but as a communication and governance challenge with profound implications for how societies function and how truth itself is constructed and contested.

The Age of Influence should mirror the nature of communication itself in the digital age: non-linear, networked, and subject to constant revision and reinterpretation. There should not be imposition of a single narrative but to make visible the threads that often remain unseen, the communication beneath the communication, the mechanisms by which meaning is made and contested.

A balance must be maintained between contemporary reflections and timeless insights. Legacy communication systems and emerging trends are placed side by side, allowing for comparisons, contrasts, and synthesis. This balance proves vital for understanding communication as both craft and strategic discipline, one that evolves technically while remaining fundamentally concerned with human perception, emotion, and meaning-making.

In positioning communication not merely as a profession or academic field but as a form of influence, memory, and under *The Age of Influence,* as a central argument for why understanding these dynamics matters beyond specialist circles. Whether through headlines, campaigns, films, speeches, or strategic silence, narratives move nations. They shape what is heard, what is remembered, and what is carried forward.

As the pace of change accelerates and information ecosystems grow ever more complex, the task of reflection becomes more critical, not to slow down progress but to anchor it. *The Age of Influence* offers itself as one such anchor: a curated collection of moments and meanings, bound by the belief that communication is not peripheral to change but central to it.

2025: The Year Indian Cinema Stopped Arriving and Started Belonging

For a long time, Indian cinema existed inside a language of anticipation. We spoke of it as an industry perpetually "on the brink", of global recognition, of serious critical legitimacy, of finally being understood beyond stereotypes. Every festival screening was framed as a breakthrough, every foreign review treated as a moment of validation. 2025 quietly dismantled that waiting-room narrative. This was not a year of arrival announcements or chest-thumping milestones. It was the year Indian cinema simply occupied space, steadily, confidently, and without explanation.

What changed most noticeably was posture. Indian films in 2025 did not travel with footnotes. They did not explain their politics, translate their emotional grammar, or dilute their cultural specificity to feel accessible. They trusted audiences to meet them where they were. That trust showed up most clearly on the global festival circuit. Indian presence this year was not limited to the number of films screened, but extended into positions of influence and permanence. When Payal Kapadia sat on the Cannes jury, it mattered not because of visibility alone, but because it signalled a comfort with Indian filmmakers as arbiters of cinematic taste, not merely participants seeking approval.

Equally telling was the way Indian cinema's past was treated alongside its present. The international showcasing of restored Indian classics, including Sholay, was not nostalgia packaged for applause. Restoration is canon-making. It is a statement that a film belongs to world cinema's long memory, not just to national sentiment. When such films are restored, screened, and discussed in global spaces, they are no longer curios from another industry; they become reference points. In 2025, Indian cinema was doing two things at once, producing new work and securing its archival legitimacy.

The contemporary films that travelled this year reflected a similar confidence. Neeraj Ghaywan's Homebound, which circulated prominently on the international circuit and later became India's official Oscars submission, did not announce itself as a "social film" or an export-ready morality tale. It was restrained, intimate, and unafraid of quietness, qualities that would once have been considered risky for an Indian film abroad. That it was received on its own terms signalled a shift in how Indian storytelling is read globally. Indian cinema no longer needed to be loud to be heard.

This broadening of India's cinematic identity was visible elsewhere too. The Indian presence at TIFF's landmark 50th edition spanned new political cinema, auteur-driven work, and restorations, offering not a single narrative but a portfolio. At Venice, Anupama Roy's Best Director win in the Orizzonti section carried a different weight altogether. These were not isolated triumphs; they suggested repeatable pathways into the global ecosystem. Indian cinema in 2025 did not feel like a guest appearance. It felt embedded.

Back home, the relationship between audiences and the big screen continued to evolve in telling ways. Theatrical cinema did not fade in 2025, but it became more intentional. Going to the movies increasingly felt like an event rather than a habit. This was visible at both ends of the spectrum, from the reverent reception to restored classics to the appetite for unapologetically large, star-driven spectacles. Films like Dhurandhar, positioned squarely as a big-screen experience, reaffirmed why theatres still matter. In an era where almost everything eventually finds its way to streaming, such films reminded audiences that scale, sound, and collective energy cannot be replicated on personal devices. The cinema hall is no longer competing with streaming platforms on volume. It is competing on experience, and in 2025, it leaned into that distinction with renewed clarity.

Everything else, mid-budget dramas, intimate character studies, experimental narratives, found a more natural home elsewhere. This was not a failure of theatres, but an evolution of format logic. The big screen reclaimed its role as a cultural occasion rather than a weekly default. In doing so, it regained a certain dignity.

Streaming, meanwhile, went through a far more unsentimental reckoning. If earlier years were marked by expansion and optimism, 2025 was defined by consolidation and realism. The merger of JioCinema and Disney+Hotstar into JioHotstar fundamentally reshaped India's OTT power structure. Combined with cricket's gravitational pull, especially the IPL, it signalled a move away from growth-at-all-costs towards control, monetisation, and scale. The shift from free streaming to hybrid access models made one thing clear: platforms were no longer chasing eyeballs alone, but sustainable revenue.

Advertising, once treated as a necessary evil for premium platforms, returned unapologetically to the centre. Prime Video's decision to introduce limited ads in India, with an optional paid upgrade for ad-free viewing, reflected a broader industry acknowledgement. Subscription fatigue is real. Disposable incomes are finite. Attention is fractured. Ad-supported tiers are no longer a compromise; they are infrastructure. Streaming in 2025 stopped pretending it could exist in a financial vacuum.

Telecom-led bundling became another quiet but telling shift. Aggregated OTT packs weren't just about convenience; they reflected changing viewer psychology. Indian audiences are pragmatic. They want value, simplicity, and flexibility. Platforms that recognised this behavioural truth adapted. Those that didn't struggled to justify their price tags. At the same time, Netflix doubled down on India not merely as a consumer market, but as a production hub, investing in diverse stories across formats, genres, and languages rather than chasing a single viral hit.

What stood out was how OTT platforms finally began behaving as if India is not one audience, but many. Sports continued to anchor mass engagement, but scripted content diversified in quieter, more confident ways. Regional stories, genre experiments, and long-form narratives were allowed to breathe. The obsession with finding "the next big thing" gave way to building libraries that reflect the country's contradictions.

Perhaps most importantly, the adversarial framing of cinema versus streaming began to dissolve. Festivals fed prestige into theatres, theatres fed visibility into streaming, and streaming fed risk-taking back into cinema. The question was no longer where a film should exist, but where it made the most sense. Format became a creative decision, not a hierarchy.

Taken together, the shifts across celluloid and OTT point to a larger truth. Indian cinema is no longer negotiating its place in a global order designed elsewhere. It is participating in shaping that order. It has learnt that influence comes not from imitation, but from confidence in its own storytelling grammar. It has also learnt that technology does not replace culture, it tests it, monetises it, stretches it, and occasionally forces it to grow up.

2025 may not be remembered for one defining film or a single dramatic moment. It will be remembered as a year of quiet consolidation, of voice, presence, and intent. A year when Indian cinema stopped asking what the world wanted from it, and started showing the world who it already was. And in a crowded global cultural landscape, that kind of self-assured clarity may be the most powerful statement of all.

Redrawing India's cinematic future

As the 56th International Film Festival of India (IFFI) came to a close in Goa, there was a sense that something larger than the event itself had just taken place. Not just a celebration of cinema, but a redefinition of what India means to the world of storytelling. The applause that rang out during the closing ceremony wasn't only for the award winners or the mesmerising cultural performances. It was for the quiet but unmistakable realisation that Indian cinema, in all its chaotic, colourful, multilingual glory, is no longer knocking on the door of the global stage, it has already walked in. Over nine days, the festival transformed Goa into a pulsating creative laboratory.

From the majestic red-carpet arrivals to the spontaneous, soul-stirring conversations between filmmakers from Iran and Assam, Slovenia and Kerala, it was a reminder that cinema continues to be one of the rare forces that can hold contradictions, commercial and experimental, local and global, ancient and futuristic, within a single frame. What made IFFI 2025 unforgettable wasn't just its scale, or even its selection of films. It was the confidence with which India projected itself. Not as a country seeking approval, but as a country defining the terms of engagement.

Take, for instance, the WAVES Film Bazaar, which this year generated a staggering Rs 1,050 crore in business. This isn't merely a record, it's a statement. India is no longer just a location for film shoots or a market for finished products. It's a co-production powerhouse, a breeding ground for emerging talent, and an investment-worthy ecosystem for anyone looking to bet on the future of global entertainment. With participation from over 77 countries, WAVES positioned India as a serious player not only in content creation but in the business of culture. In a world rapidly turning to soft power as a marker of geopolitical influence, this matters more than we acknowledge.

And yet, the business deals, the market numbers, and the pitch sessions were only part of the story. The emotional centre of IFFI 2025 lay in the stories being told and the storytellers being discovered. The Golden Peacock went to Skin of Youth, a Vietnamese film that dared to be tender and confrontational in the same breath. Santosh Davakhar's Marathi gem Gondhal felt like an ode to the oral traditions of India's heartland while pulsating with the structure and surprise of modern theatre. Meanwhile, Karan Singh Tyagi's Kesari Chapter 2 showed that even mainstream Indian stories could compete on the merit of vision and voice. This collision of cultures, genres, and perspectives, curated with care, not just diversity for diversity's sake, was proof that IFFI is curating possibility.

This edition also did something that most festivals hesitate to do: it blended legacy with innovation, emotion with technology. While the world paid homage to cinematic legends like Dharmendra and Rajinikanth, whose 50-year reign in Indian cinema was celebrated with thunderous applause, IFFI boldly planted its feet into the future. The AI Film Festival and CinemAI Hackathon weren't just footnotes; they were provocations. They asked what happens when storytelling and machine intelligence collide, not to replace human creativity, but to expand its vocabulary. For young creators, this wasn't theoretical. It was an invitation to reimagine the act of filmmaking itself.

And with the launch of the Indian Institute of Creative Technology (IICT) in

Mumbai, that reimagination now has an institutional anchor. India isn't just nurturing its film-makers, it's training its future disruptors. What emerged most clearly was a deeper ideological shift. For the first time, perhaps, IFFI felt less like a mirror reflecting global cinema trends and more like a prism refracting Indian ones. Fifty films by women directors weren't programmed as a special category, they were the main event. Accessibility wasn't an afterthought, it was embedded, from Indian Sign Language interpreters to divyang-friendly measures across the festival.

The spirit of Vasudhaiva Kutumbakam was not simply echoed in speeches, it was visible in the warmth with which filmmakers from Estonia and Iran, Slovenia and Nigeria, were embraced, engaged, and elevated. There was also something poetic about how the programming honoured the centenary legacies of visionaries like Guru Dutt, Raj Khosla, and Ritwik Ghatak, even as it introduced new voices whose names we may be hearing for the next hundred years. IFFI didn't just screen films, it held space for memory. In a world racing to the next scroll, the next trend, the next dopamine hit, this festival dared to slow down. It invited us to linger. To sit still inside a story.

To breathe with a character, to ache for an ending, to remember. That in itself felt radical. In a time when content is consumed faster than it's made, here was a place that asked nothing of us but attention, and gave back emotion in return. Every frame was a pause. Every applause, a collective exhale. And in the quiet between the lights and the language, something else became clear: IFFI 2025 did not just position India on the global cinema map; it changed how the world orientated itself towards Indian storytelling. Not as a moment of curiosity or a cultural detour, but as a destination. For decades, partnerships with India were often transactional or tinted with exoticism. We were the location, the backdrop, the colour palette.

But now, those frames are shifting. India is stepping in not just as a collaborator, but as a co-creator, someone who has equal skin in the game, equal imagination, equal ownership. And the magic of this shift isn't confined to glossy studios or scripted boardrooms. It's happening in writing rooms in Bhopal and editing suites in Trivandrum, in the minds of students in Pune and storytellers in Shillong. Something sacred is moving. And it's moving forward. The hunger, raw, restless, radiant, was visible on the faces of young CMOT creators pitching their stories to global producers. It echoed in the applause for Bandish Bandits Season 2 winning Best OTT Series, a homegrown show that made classical music mainstream again.

And it was perhaps most visible in the silence that followed the screening of A Useful Ghost, the haunting Thai film that closed the festival. As the credits rolled, the room stayed quiet. Not because it was unsure how to react, but because it knew it had just witnessed something unforgettable. That's what IFFI did. It reminded us that cinema still has the power to leave us speechless. So, what does all this mean for the future? It means that India is no longer emerging, it has emerged. Not just as a market or a location, but as a lens through which the world will increasingly want to see itself. It means that Indian creators are not just inheriting a legacy, they are inventing one. The curtain may have fallen on IFFI 2025, but its echoes will reverberate for years. In the deals signed, the stories seeded, the collaborations initiated, and in the quiet revolution of a nation ready to tell its story not just to itself, but to the world.

IFFI in its future edition needs to position the five mantras guiding cinema globally – Collaboration, C o op eration, C o ordination, Convergence and Cohesion, the hub for creativity, global impression offering the shades of soft-power impact on the festival landscape. IFFI needs to reinforce fresh thinking, perspectives and a new stream of narrative building and knowledge sharing. The 57th edition of IFFI should keep in mind the objective of placing its influence on hearts and minds of cinephiles, giving a bigger push to quality, character and relatability of movies in the film festival circuit. It needs to carry forward the global impact of the "Namaste Gesture" of Oscars in 2025, giving the world a new mantra of inclusivity and the platform to bring creators and creativity together.

Framing India's AI governance: India's vision and voice

Dear reader, by now you must be convinced on how artificial intelligence is weaving into India's social fabric. While generative AI continues to provoke debate over its disruptive potential, one consensus remains: AI is here to stay. As India races to define the rules and ethics of artificial intelligence, the real battleground isn't only in policy documents or technical standards-it's in communication. How governments frame AI, how industry markets it, how media reports it, and how citizens discuss it on WhatsApp or in local languages all shape public trust and understanding. India's AI journey is a high-stakes narrative of ambition meets reality.

India's AI adoption unfolds as a government-orchestrated epic, blending visionary blueprints with practical enablers to empower the masses. At its core lies the Honourable Prime Minister's vision of "AI for All," articulated in the November 2025 India AI Governance Guidelines, which positions AI as a force multiplier for Viksit Bharat by 2047. This framework builds on foundational initiatives like the National Strategy for AI, emphasizing responsible AI for social empowerment through applications in rural healthcare diagnostics, localized education, and farmer-centric climate resilience tools. "Safe & Trusted AI" pillar, a cornerstone of the IndiaAI Mission, democratizes access by investing in foundational ecosystem layers-compute resources, data-sharing platforms, and widespread skilling to counter global concentrations of AI capabilities. Complementing this are Digital Public Infrastructure (DPI) successes such as Aadhaar, UPI, and DigiLocker, now evolving into multilingual interfaces like Bhashini, which tailor AI to India's linguistic tapestry of 22 official languages and beyond. From a communications standpoint, these initiatives craft an uplifting narrative of inclusion, yet they demand vigilant storytelling to address risks like misinformation and biases.

The industry landscape injects vitality into AI's evolution, positioning it as a driver of widespread transformation across diverse applications. Businesses in various fields are encouraged to harness digital public infrastructure for expansive outreach, alongside efforts to broaden availability of essential data and processing resources, drawing in capital and spurring creative advancements. Operational advice emphasizes embracing self-initiated standards, issuing regular disclosures on practices, and employing combined technical and regulatory strategies to address potential downsides-aligning implementations in areas like health services, public administration, and more with core ethical considerations. This domain's contribution is essential in bridging conceptual strategies with tangible outcomes, though narrative hurdles persist: Exuberance surrounding advanced generative technologies requires balancing with clear revelations that reinforce societal assurance, averting any slowdown in momentum.

Academic and research contributions infuse intellectual rigor and emphasize capacity building to bridge gaps. Programs for education, skilling, and training are prioritized to empower individuals, heighten awareness of AI's opportunities and risks, and cultivate a workforce attuned to ethical imperatives. Institutions like those under the Technology & Policy Expert Committee (TPEC) are tasked with informing standards, reflecting a narrative shift toward human-centric design. Yet, from a comms lens, academia's voice often remains siloed; amplifying research on algorithmic fairness through accessible dialogues could enrich national storytelling, aligning with the “People First” principle.

India's AI narrative is shaped by its vast social and cultural diversity, demanding governance that balances scale with equity while avoiding biases that could deepen divides across languages, regions, and communities. As AI enters classrooms, farms, and public services, communications must demystify how these systems work-translating probabilistic algorithms and emerging risks into relatable, empowering stories that counter fears of deepfakes, surveillance, or discrimination. India's “jugaad” ingenuity sits alongside cultural caution about powerful technologies, making it vital for ethical frameworks and public narratives to evolve with new breakthroughs, as stressed in ongoing government-industry-civil society dialogues. In this context, vernacular multimedia campaigns become essential, turning abstract ethical concerns into human-centred messages that embody an approach to AI governance that is truly "Understandable by Design."

Public and private sectors in India collaborate as key architects in advancing AI, blending governmental coordination with industry agility to drive ethical and inclusive growth. The public sector takes the lead in setting strategic directions through a coordinated, multi-agency structure that spans central ministries, specialized regulators, and advisory groups. This ensures a unified push toward building robust AI ecosystems, with high-level bodies focusing on overarching policy alignment and technical safeguards. Sector-specific enforcers maintain oversight on compliance, while expert committees provide ongoing guidance on emerging challenges, emphasizing human-centered approaches and risk-aware deployments. Such integration fosters an environment where public investments in foundational resources like data platforms and computational power directly support widespread adoption, particularly in critical areas such as healthcare and agriculture.

India's early AI policy efforts have evolved from broad strategic visions to targeted, adaptable frameworks, laying groundwork for responsible scaling. Initial national strategies focused on sector-specific applications, such as improving public services and economic productivity, while subsequent missions emphasized foundational investments in computing infrastructure and skill enhancement programs. The latest comprehensive guidelines, released in early November 2025, introduce a structured approach across enabling, regulatory, and oversight domains, including tailored risk evaluation tools and phased implementation timelines. Short-term measures prioritize institutional setups and voluntary adoption mechanisms, medium-term steps involve standard publications and experimental regulatory environments, and long-term plans call for ecosystem reviews and legislative updates to handle new capabilities.

These interventions demonstrate notable effectiveness in promoting innovation without stifling progress. The emphasis on flexible, evidence-based adjustments has facilitated quicker responses to real-world issues like data biases and security vulnerabilities, contributing to broader trust in AI systems. However, gaps remain in enforcement consistency and public awareness, with calls for enhanced training initiatives and transparent liability structures to strengthen outcomes. Overall, the policies' pragmatic blend of voluntary and mandatory elements has positioned India to harness AI's potential for inclusive development, though sustained communication efforts are essential to amplify their reach and address lingering adoption barriers in diverse contexts.

IFFI 2025: A Celebration of Influence, Innovation, and India

Every edition of IFFI has been a huge leap forward for cinema. The platform has served as the perfect jugalbandi of creativity, excellence, diversity, insights, ideas, and innovation. Every year, it gives the image and brand of India an extra punch, reinforcing our soft power and global cultural imprint. IFFI offers cinephiles a vibrant, living architecture of cinema that one can relish, absorb, and get lost in. No other festival in the world quite matches the matrix of variety, the interweaving of the old and the contemporary, the grand and the intimate. It is a cinematic sanctum where legacy breathes beside experimentation. The idea of wholesome entertainment expands in meaning each year, as IFFI Goa transforms into a City of Cinema, its streets echoing with storylines, its venues pulsing with the heartbeat of storytelling through the lens of creators whose instinct for deep thought is unprecedented.

The festival's sister platform, the Waves Bazaar, reinforces the power of collaboration in the evolving landscape of filmmaking. More than a market, it is a cultural junction for filmmakers, producers, sales agents, and dreamers, an intellectual and artistic space where ideas meet investment, and stories cross borders. Together, IFFI and Waves Film Bazaar capture the contours of New India, a nation that tells stories not just with emotion but with cutting-edge technology, market wisdom, and strategic global positioning. NFDC continues to highlight cinema not merely as entertainment, but as a vehicle of progress, diplomacy, and development, a shared language of partnership among nations, makers, and markets.

This year's 56th edition of IFFI stands tall in what can only be called The Age Of Influence, an age where cinema is no longer passive but powerful, interactive, and increasingly global. And in this new age, IFFI has outdone itself. The 2025 edition turns the spotlight onto women and emerging talent like never before, with over 50 films directed by women and more than 50 debut features showcased in the international section. Five Indian debut features will compete for the coveted Best Debut Director of an Indian Feature Film award, carrying a cash prize of ₹5 lakhs. In an age of digital storytelling, IFFI also embraces the OTT wave with a dedicated Best Web Series Award, selected from 30 submissions and awarding ₹10 lakhs to the winning creators. Parallel to this, the Creative Minds of Tomorrow (CMOT) programme has surged in popularity, with a staggering 799 entries this year and 124 selected participants representing 13 crafts, including three new ones. With the ShortsTV 48-hour challenge pushing creative limits, the festival has become an incubator of tomorrow's auteurs.

The Waves Film Bazaar too has grown into South Asia's most dynamic co-production and distribution hub. In its 19th edition, the Bazaar will present over 300 projects across segments like the Screenwriters Lab, Viewing Room Library, Market Screenings, and the

Co-Production Market, which will spotlight 22 feature films and 5 documentaries, offering $20,000 in grants to three winners. The WFBR (Waves Film Bazaar Recommends) section will feature 22 remarkable titles across 14 languages and 4 countries, highlighting a wave of bold debut filmmakers. Its Knowledge Series will feature interactive industry sessions, pitch panels, and state and country showcases, while a dedicated Tech Pavilion will showcase frontier technologies in VFX, CGI, and animation in collaboration with five major players, making Goa the heart of global cinema tech for the week. Networking events will foster crucial partnerships between producers, distributors, festival programmers, and financial stakeholders, turning stories into deals, and scripts into global journeys.

As the lights come up on the big screen, IFFI 2025 will host 21 riveting masterclasses and panel discussions at Kala Academy, led by cinematic luminaries such as Aamir Khan, Anupam Kher, Vidhu Vinod Chopra, Ravi Varman, Suhasini Maniratnam, Pete Draper, Christopher Charles Corbould OBE, Sreekar Prasad, Bobby Deol, and Khushboo Sundar. These conversations will delve into everything from acting in the digital era to the role of cinema in promoting peace, from theatre acting to the integration of AI and VFX in modern filmmaking. Not just technical training but soul-stirring dialogues will emerge, about art, relevance, responsibility, and vision.

Adding another jewel to its crown, IFFI introduces a vibrant new cultural layer this year, IFFIESTA. From November 21 to 24, IFFIESTA 2025 will offer four evenings of live music, theatre, and storytelling, bridging the magic of cinema with the magic of the stage. Designed to be participatory and joyful, IFFIESTA will be a festival within the festival, a celebration of sound, stagecraft, and shared experience where emerging artists and seasoned performers meet in creative synergy. Accessibility too remains a non-negotiable ethos. From multilingual dubbing and audio descriptions to sign-language interpreters, IFFI ensures that every story can reach every eye and ear, with five key venues, INOX Panjim, INOX Porvorim, Maquinez Palace, Z-Square Samrat Ashok, and Ravindra Bhavan Madgaon, and open-air screenings at Miramar, Fatorda, and Anjuna beaches offering immersive experiences to cinephiles of every background.

This year's International Jury, chaired by visionary director Rakeysh Omprakash Mehra, brings together global voices: Graeme Clifford (Australia), Remi Adefarasin (UK), Katharina Schüttler (Germany), and Chandran Rutnam (Sri Lanka). They will judge a line-up that features some of the most decorated films of the year, including It Was Just An Accident (Palme d'Or, Cannes), Father Mother Sister Brother (Golden Lion, Venice), Dreams (Golden Bear,

Berlin), Sirât (Grand Jury Prize, Cannes), The Message (Silver Bear, Berlin), No Other Choice (People's Choice, TIFF), Gloaming in Luomu (Best Film, Busan), and Fiume o Morte! (Tiger Award, IFFR). These films reaffirm IFFI's standing as a truly global platform where excellence is not just showcased, but debated, discovered, and honoured.

For me, having served as Festival Director for four editions, every moment of IFFI has been a dream sprint. From the world's first hybrid film festival during COVID to our Oscar-winning selections, from navigating the OTT blitz to curating programming that the world emulated, this journey has been as exhilarating as it was humbling. And while I may be missing this edition for personal reasons, I know IFFI will continue its triumphant run, bolder and brighter than ever. Because in Goa, cinema is not an industry or an event, it's a celebration of consciousness, creativity, and country. And IFFI 2025, in every sense of the word, is a festival of influence, imagination, and India.

Rescuing and restoring the soul of Indian cinema

Cinema is more than moving images on a screen. It is memory, imagination, and history intertwined. Each film captures a moment in time, a reflection of who we were, what we dreamt of, and how we saw the world. Yet, like all fragile memories, films fade too. Neglect, decay, and time have already erased countless treasures from India's cinematic past. Recently, I came across a full-page advertisement of an upcoming event organised by the Indian Cinema Heritage Foundation's one-day symposium on cinema, 'Future of Memories', and I jumped with joy.

As someone who truly cherishes films, I believe there's no better way to honour our cinematic past than by bringing its classics back to life through restoration.

Every restored frame is a resurrection of history. Film preservation is not just about saving celluloid; it's about protecting a piece of cultural identity. When we preserve a film, we preserve the artistry, emotion, and vision of the people who created it. We preserve their struggles, their experiments, and their reflections of society. Each reel becomes a time capsule of fashion, architecture, speech, and values that defined an era. For India, with its rich and varied film traditions across languages and regions, preservation holds even greater importance. Our cinema has chronicled the nation's changing landscape from the hopes of independence to the complexities of modern life. Losing these films would mean losing our collective story.

Preservation allows us to revisit that legacy, to study the evolution of storytelling, and to appreciate the craftsmanship of the filmmakers who came before us. What makes this moment particularly exciting is how technology has transformed the possibilities of film restoration. Advanced digital tools now allow experts to clean, repair, and even reconstruct damaged films with remarkable precision. Scratches are removed, colors are revived, and sound is restored to its original depth. This technological progress has not only made restoration more accessible but has also helped Indian cinema regain its rightful place on the world stage.

Restored classics are now being showcased at major international festivals, sparking renewed appreciation for the depth and artistry of our cinematic tradition. A remarkable example of this is the restoration of Shyam Benegal's Manthan, a project undertaken by the Film Heritage Foundation (FHF) with support from the Gujarat Cooperative Milk Marketing Federation Ltd. (Amul). Released in 1976, Manthan (meaning The Churning) remains one of Indian cinema's most powerful depictions of social transformation. The film tells the story of Dr Rao, a young veterinary doctor played by Girish Karnad, who works with rural farmers to establish a milk cooperative.

The film's ensemble, featuring Smita Patil, Naseeruddin Shah, and Amrish Puri, brings to life a story that is as much about community empowerment as it is about individual conviction. What made Manthan historic was not just its theme, but its making. The film was crowdfunded by over five lakh farmers who each contributed two rupees to bring the project to life, making it India's first people-funded film. In many ways, its recent restoration carries forward that same collective spirit. When Manthan was restored and screened at the Cannes Classics section of the Cannes Film Festival, it was not merely an aesthetic triumph; it was a reaffirmation of how deeply cinema is woven into India's cultural fabric.

The restored version shimmered with new life, allowing international audiences to experience not just the story but the legacy of India's rural revolution and its cinema's humanistic power. Restoring a film is like restoring a piece of history that can continue to inspire future generations. For students of cinema, these restored classics serve as invaluable archives of technique, storytelling, and cultural representation. They reveal how Indian filmmakers responded to their times, how they framed questions of gender, caste, modernity, and identity through their art.

Film preservation, therefore, is not nostalgia-driven; it is future-oriented. It ensures that the creative achievements of the past can continue to educate and inspire. It also brings inclusivity to the narrative of Indian cinema, giving long-overlooked regional and independent films the space they deserve in the national and global conversation. Initiatives such as ‘Future of Memories’ play a vital role in nurturing awareness and appreciation for film heritage. They remind us that saving films is not the responsibility of experts alone; it is a shared cultural duty. Such forums also spark a new consciousness among the audience, encouraging people to look at films not just as entertainment, but as historical artifacts that carry our collective imagination forward.

They highlight how preserving cinema is akin to preserving a nation's memory. Organisations like the Film Heritage Foundation (FHF) have also been instrumental in safeguarding India's cinematic treasures. Through meticulous restoration, digitisation, and archival efforts, they have ensured that old classic films are not lost to time. Their work allows audiences in 2025 to witness these films as they were meant to be seen— preserved yet reinvigorated by modern technology. Since film reels deteriorate with time, digital preservation is paramount to save India's rich cinema history for future generations.

Preserving films demands vision, technical expertise, and resources, but above all, it requires love. The work of organisations like the Indian Cinema

Heritage Foundation and the Film Heritage Foundation stands as a testament to this passion. Their tireless efforts to rescue and restore India's cinematic gems are a reminder that cultural heritage cannot be taken for granted. Films may be fragile, but their stories are enduring. Through preservation, restoration, and dialogue, we ensure that the soul of Indian cinema continues to live, breathe, and inspire not just as history, but as a living, evolving legacy.

As modernisation accelerates, the desire to stay connected to cultural roots grows stronger. Old films serve as powerful reminders of India's artistic traditions, moral values, and storytelling craft. They provide a bridge between the past and the present, allowing audiences to reflect on where cinema has come from while contemplating its future. The preservation era is not just about nostalgia. It is a celebration of identity, heritage, and an enduring love for stories that have stood the test of time.

People-First Framework: Centre Chalks Out Inclusive Strategy With AI Governance Guidelines

The Centre recently released the AI Governance Guidelines, focusing on trusted AI innovation. It is a pragmatic approach, and now the onus is on the policymakers and stakeholders to maintain the momentum

In the age of instant communication, infodemics, fakery, and technology-enabled communication architecture, AI has become a trigger push phenomenon. While it holds immense promise to change the ecosystem, it is important that the architecture and framework governing AI implementation are clearly outlined with specific touch points, objectives, and guidelines, in order to ensure an inclusive future.

Taking the lead, the Government of India (GoI) recently released the 'AI Governance Guidelines', focusing on trusted AI innovation.

The key objective of this endeavour is to ensure a seamless last-mile connectivity and impact — one that ensures benefits, satisfaction, and empowerment for every citizen of the country. It is an honest attempt to ensure that people embrace this technological innovation to address critical issues in their lives. It positions safety as the mantra of AI implementation.

It is truly pragmatic, as it recognises the pitfalls in implementing such a bold, diversified, multi-stakeholder policy. The document and its guiding principles provide a framework that would be resilient in the future for governance and institutional viability.

Keeping The AI Balance

At the same time, the model will ensure the balance between AI innovation, accountability, progress, and growth.

The guidelines are centred around the "People-First" approach, ensuring that the application is sectorally beneficial to the citizens; and, thereby, AI plays a key role in the path towards Viksit Bharat 2047.

The document also lays the framework for India to be a leading global player, conscious of the challenges confronting the governance model. The framework outlined in the document is an end-to-end approach. It follows the mantra of "Whole of Government

Approach", establishing a platform that believes in equity, inclusiveness, affordability, and accessibility. The framework is unique as it takes into account the diversity of the country by providing a foundation that addresses the needs of the people and the stakeholders alike. The objective is to build an ethical and technical framework that internalises the "Idea of India" in its march towards Viksit Bharat 2047.

The "Guiding Principles or Sutras" of the guidelines are: Trust is the foundation of the entire approach; it underscores the need for systems that citizens can rely on without hesitation. The philosophy of "People-First" calls for a human-centric design that prioritises user experience and societal impact. The policy places innovation over restraint, encouraging responsible innovation that does not stifle creativity, but instead channels it for meaningful outcomes.

Fairness and equity remain at the heart of the policy, ensuring that AI benefits reach every section of society, and that no one is left behind in this technological shift. The principle of accountability strengthens this promise by making sure responsibilities are clearly defined at every stage of the AI lifecycle, so that citizens know who is answerable for what.

AI That Is Easy To Access

The framework also emphasises the need for AI systems to be easy to understand, designed in a way that users, regulators, and citizens can navigate without confusion.

And, ultimately, the policy anchors itself in safety, resilience, and sustainability, building AI systems that can withstand shocks, adapt to new challenges, and continue serving people reliably even in moments of uncertainty.

AI Summit 2026

The upcoming India AI Summit 2026 will be the moment when India turns global conversations into concrete action.

Rather than simply participating in the worldwide dialogue on AI governance, India wants to help shape it, offering a vision that is practical, inclusive, and deeply connected to the country's own developmental journey.

The Summit's broader mission ties directly with India's goal of building one of the world's most people-centric and widely accessible AI ecosystems.

The event will centre around three simple but powerful pillars:

- talent,
- technology,
- trust

On talent, India is focusing on preparing its people for the future, expanding AI skilling across universities, technical institutes, and vocational platforms so learners, at every level, can access emerging opportunities. On technology, the Summit will spotlight how AI can work hand-in-hand with India's Digital Public Infrastructure, making everyday services more multilingual, secure, and accessible.

A major focus will also be on the safe and responsible use of frontier AI models. Strengthening oversight, improving evaluation methods, and developing harmonised safety standards are key steps India plans to take as part of its forward-looking governance blueprint.

At the same time, the Summit hopes to move AI innovation beyond the big metros by supporting Tier-2 and Tier-3 cities as new hubs for experimentation, research, and entrepreneurship.

On the global stage, India plans to champion cross-border testbeds and stronger partnerships across the Global South, creating shared spaces to build, test, and deploy trusted AI solutions. The Summit will also look at how AI can help governments work more efficiently.

The India AI Summit 2026 aims to chart a path that is both ambitious and grounded. It reflects a belief that AI must always be used in ways that uplift people, strengthen communities, and support India's long-term aspiration of becoming a Viksit Bharat by 2047.

Celebrating the Geniuses of Laughter: Honouring the Craft of Comedy in Bollywood

In the vast, emotional, and ever-evolving tapestry of Hindi cinema, comedy has often been the thread that holds everything together. It's the reprieve between drama, the levity that offsets tragedy, the rhythm that gives films their human pulse. And yet, it is the one craft most taken for granted. The passing of two stalwarts, Asrani and Satish Shah, within days of each other, reminds us that true comedic brilliance is rare, irreplaceable, and worthy of reverence. And it makes one thing heartbreakingly clear: we are slowly losing the artists who once defined what it meant to truly, deeply, joyfully laugh.

GovardhanAsrani, forever etched in our memories as the outrageously funny jailor in Sholay, had a way of walking the tightrope between chaos and control like nobody else. Over five decades and hundreds of films later, you realise, he wasn't just cracking jokes, he was conducting an orchestra. His characters may have leaned into the ridiculous, but they were never hollow. There was always a clever glint behind the madness, a rhythm in his timing that made even the silliest lines feel strangely sophisticated. And then there's

Satish Shah, effortlessly iconic, joyfully unpredictable.

The man played 55 characters in Yeh Jo HaiZindagi and made each one feel like someone you've met at a family wedding. As Indravadan in Sarabhai vs Sarabhai, he didn't just steal scenes, he was the scene. No gimmicks, no noise, just sharp timing, dry wit, and the kind of delivery that'll hit your witty bone in an instant and make the moment unforgettable. It's important to understand that what these legends did was no accident. Comedy is hard. Far harder than it looks. To land a joke isn't just about the line, it's about the beat before it, the silence after it, the expression you wear when you say it, and the truth you don't say at all.

It demands the precision of a musician, the instincts of a dramatist, and the heart of a poet. While the world often glorifies method actors and tragic heroes for their intensity, it is the comedians, the true ones, who have the most challenging job: to connect, disarm, and uplift, often in a matter of seconds. Great comedy is not loud. It is control. It is listening. It is generosity. It's the rare ability to shape a moment not just for yourself but for your scene partner, your audience, and for the film's rhythm itself. Asrani and Satish Shah weren't just brilliant actors, they were part of a long, golden lineage of artists who taught us that comedy in Indian cinema was never just a filler between plot points. It was the plot. It was culture, commentary, catharsis.

It was survival. They carried forward a legacy built by giants like Johnny Walker, Mehmood, and Kader Khan, each of whom redefined what it meant to make people laugh, and more importantly, why we laugh. Johnny Walker, with his famously slurred delivery and wobbly walk, didn't simply spoof the drunkard, he gave him soul. He made that character relatable, even endearing, in a way that never felt exploitative.

There was a sweetness in his timing, a twinkle in his eye that told you he wasn't just chasing laughs, he was inviting you to feel for the man behind the joke. Then there was Mehmood, the eternal chameleon, whose range was almost terrifying. In one scene he could be ridiculous, laugh-out-loud funny, and in the next, he could shatter your heart with a single glance. He played the fool, the dreamer, the sidekick, the father, the everyman, and through all of them, he gave us empathy dressed in humour.

And Kader Khan. He was something else entirely. Not just a comedian, but a writer, a philosopher in disguise. His dialogues were clever, yes, but they were also wise. You laughed, and then the meaning would hit you a moment later. He didn't just tell jokes, he built punchlines that doubled as life advice, as critique, as poetic observation. His words still echo across generations because they were layered with meaning, not just laughter. Let's not forget the comedic powerhouses who redefined presence, tone, and timing in their own right. TunTun turned every stereotype she was boxed into into a weapon, and then turned the weapon into a joke. ArunaIrani and Farida Jalal brought warmth and sharpness in equal measure, making even a one-line comeback feel like a scene-stealer.

Archana Puran Singh proved that being loud doesn't mean being shallow, it means owning the moment like no one else can. RatnaPathak Shah as Maya Sarabhai delivered insults so elegantly, you almost wanted to thank her. SeemaPahwa, with her effortless realism, turned domestic chaos into pure gold. And in the world of live comedy, Bharti Singh has held her own in rooms that were never built to include her in the first place, rewriting the rules, one punchline at a time. These artists were never "comic relief." They were the relief. They were the pulse that steadied you when everything else in the story grew too heavy. And that's what people often fail to understand about comedy, it's not just about being funny. It's about knowing when to be funny, how much to give, and when to stop.

It's about reading the room, the rhythm of the scene, and somehow making everyone watching feel like you're in sync with their emotion. Today, in a world overflowing with content, where every second person can stitch a meme or crack a viral joke, it's easy to forget what true mastery looks like. Anyone can be loud. Anyone can shout or make faces or force a laugh. But to be profoundly, genuinely funny, the kind of funny that gets under your skin and stays there, the kind of funny that people quote twenty years later, that takes genius. That takes timing. That takes years of failure, of trial, of being laughed at before you learn to make them laugh with you. Asrani and Satish Shah did exactly that. Their roles may not have always been the protagonists, but they were often the scenes we remembered most. The lines we waited for. The pauses that made the punchline soar.

And honestly, isn't that the true test of greatness? When you're not the lead on paper, but you become the lead in memory. Let's think about how many times we've rewatched those old films and found ourselves smiling before the joke even lands, just at the sight of them on screen. That anticipation, that affection, that trust, that's not easy to earn. That's legacy. That's what these actors built, not just careers, but comfort. They gave us relief. They gave us rhythm. And they gave us the sacred gift of laughter that didn't talk down to us, it laughed with us. So maybe the best way we honour them now is by watching closely. Listening deeply.Laughing not just from the surface, but from the soul.And reminding ourselves, again and again, that when done right, comedy isn't escape. It's art. And the legends who mastered it? They weren't just actors. They were alchemists. The writer is a former civil servant; he writes on cinema and strategic communication.

Lines that touched a nation

It was one of those mornings when the news hits harder than your first cup of coffee. Piyush Pandey, the master craftsman of Indian advertising, has left us.

And with him goes an era when advertisements didn't just sell products but told us stories about ourselves. If advertising mirrors society, Pandey's advertisements reflected simplicity, hope and the little things that brought us joy. His work told us that India's beauty lies not in perfection but in connection. His copy was as sharp as his handlebar moustache and just as iconic. He had the rare gift of noticing the obvious and turning it into magic.

The iconic Cadbury advertisement sold that fleeting moment when a young girl danced through a cricket field, a bar of chocolate in hand, telling us, "Kuch Khaas Hai Zindagi Mein." We might be in 2025, but it still holds the same charm it did when it first came out. That one slogan made us look for joy in the ordinary. His work with the Polio campaign, "Do Boond Zindagi Ki," is perhaps the best example of advertising as a force for social good. Coupled with Amitabh Bachchan's gravitas, those four words changed behaviour across a nation. Two drops. Life itself. The simplicity was deceptive, the impact monumental. That's what happens when you understand people, not just consumers.

Pandey had a particular genius for turning mundane products into memorable characters. Take Fevicol. In addition to promoting adhesive, he developed a whole universe in which the product's potency served as the joke. A Fevicol advertisement on the back of an overcrowded bus held everyone together while they dangled precariously, defying the laws of physics. When a confused man tried to crack an egg for breakfast, he found that the hen had been pecking at Fevicol and producing eggs that were indestructible. While a hobbyist with pricey equipment watched in shock, a local fisherman used a stick to dab with FeviKwik and pluck fish straight out of the water. "Yeh Fevicol ka jod hai, tutega nahi" became a tagline for anything that could not be broken, from friendships to questionable life decisions. Then there was the little pug that became a cultural phenomenon.

The Hutch campaign showed a boy being followed everywhere by a devoted pug, quietly communicating network reliability through the simple metaphor of loyalty. The ad was so effective that an entire generation started calling pugs "the Hutch dog." That's the kind of cultural penetration that today's ad campaigns, despite their multi-platform strategies and influencer armies, struggle to achieve. Modern advertising often feels like it is written for algorithms, not people. Lines are crafted to please search engines and eventually find their way to the consumer. There is polish, but little pulse. Everyone's chasing the next viral campaign while forgetting that the best ones were rarely designed to go viral.

Advertisements today have their own rhythm, no doubt – influencer collaborations, viral trends, content that lives and dies in 24-hour cycles. Nothing wrong with that, but something feels missing. When was the last time you remembered an ad? Not just laughed at a meme or shared a reel, but actually remembered the message, the product, and how it all came together to build a brand? The iconic ads, whether it was Asian Paints' "Har Ghar Kuch Kehta Hai" or the soul-stirring "Mile Sur Mera Tumhara," had recall value that transcended their media spends. You didn't need a hundred influencer partnerships to make people remember. You needed one good insight, executed brilliantly. Pandey's copywriting was surgical. Every word earned its place.

Each punch line was a jugalbandi of ideation, rationality, human experience, and real-life situations. Compare that to today, when we are drowning in content but starving for meaning. We've got 10 different ways to say the same thing, all optimized for SEO, all sounding vaguely similar. The craft has given way to the formula. The insight has been replaced by the template. What's missing? The human touch. The cultural understanding. The patience to sit with an idea until it reveals itself. Pandey believed in people-centric advertising, and his love for cultural design thinking gave Indian advertising a global presence. Today, we're so busy chasing virality that we forget to chase truth. So here we are. The man who taught us that every home has a story, that there's something special in life, has directed his final scene. The credits are rolling, but the taglines remain, echoing across generations with unbridled enthusiasm. And as we sit here, scrolling through our algorithmically curated feeds, perhaps Pandey's greatest legacy isn't just the ads he created, but the reminder he left behind: that good storytelling never goes out of fashion. The platforms may change, the formats may evolve, but the human need for connection remains constant.

Misinformation Warfare: The New Frontline in Global Geopolitics

In today's war-tensed world, images and videos don't just go viral, they explode. Like digital bombs, they scatter shards of truth, half-truths, and outright falsehoods across borders, screens, and minds. We are living in an age where one deepfake can shatter diplomatic trust, one AI-generated image can incite unrest, and one viral headline can sabotage years of negotiation. When misinformation and fake news enter this roster of weaponry, the tragedy is compounded. What could have been a moment of resilience turns into a spectacle of doubt and chaos. The recent escalations in the Indian subcontinent stand as a burning example of this. As tensions rose, misinformation surged; fabricated visuals, misattributed videos, and misleading narratives flooded social media. But what stood out was the

Indian government's prompt and proactive response: deploying fact-check units, engaging official handles, and taking down false content in real time. It wasn't just governance; it was communication warfare.

Strategic communication in today's geopolitical space has become a battlefield of contending ideas, contrasting perceptions, diverse strategies and complex narratives.

In 2025, the framework of geopolitical landscape, has been affected by the geostrategic communication architecture. The entire ecosystem has become a "Bitter Platform of pulls and pressure", A "Tug of War" and "Slanging Match" being played out on different media formats by stakeholders whose image is at stake. The moot question is whether geostrategic communication requires overriding restraints to focus on limits of misuse of content through deep fakes, AI generated images, falsehood promotion and trigger generated perception and response. Recent events have shown that the geopolitical space is on a "24x7 Communication Alert". The buzz thereby generated has influenced the contours of core diplomatic interface and messaging structure. It has also sent warning signals that wrap around "Communication Disorder", misinformation and hyped ecosystem content. The entire communication operation is not a messaging tool, rather it is being positioned as a strategic weapon to misguide and negatively align thereby disturbing the "Information Equilibrium and Discourse".

In the good old days, geopolitics was dominated by conventional tools and channels of dissemination, bilateral interface and personal diplomacy interference to counter negative narratives, perceptions and sentiments. Today, the conventional wisdom has been overtaken by **"Communication Strikes"** which thrive on utilizing the space to destabilize, manipulate and churn unwanted crisis, narratives and unending falsehood in an era of instant communication. Policy makers and strategist grapple with the matrix of complex "**Communication Intersections**" where ground rules are not constant, thrive on fakery and "Communication Escalation" points. Any crisis that impacts geopolitics today thrives on communication disorder, imbalance and asymmetry. The lack of understanding to dissect the negative content amongst the audiences, leads to being a prey to biased hostile reporting. This has been one of the biggest obstacles to transparency in communicating the right message through the appropriate medium. Fact checking units have become the new normal of the global order. Image depiction, messaging consistency within the diplomatic landscape has suffered pitfalls due to lack of reciprocity in outlining events, issues and themes.

The Indian subcontinent witnessed this first-hand. As tension escalated, certain media outlets and social platforms were flooded with images and videos purportedly from conflict zones. Many of these were from unrelated incidents or were digitally manipulated to incite public panic. However, Indian authorities acted swiftly: real-time fact-checking, dissemination of verified updates, and coordinated efforts with social media platforms helped curb the impact. The government of India's Fact Check Unit PIB, under the aegis of I&B Ministry, played a critical role in stalling the flow of disinformation flooded in the social media space in the recent events of neighbourhood tension. The result? A temporary restoration of the information order in a region otherwise on the brink of digital chaos. The need for a new global information order is acute, arises on account of the gaps fissures that appear in the messaging and perception terrain.

Due to the deep impact of social media, every medium and tool within the geostrategic space is suffering from "Asymmetrical Dynamics". Dynamics related to information overload, overhype infodemics, lack of credibility and the growing role and interplay of non-state elements in the ecosystem.

The need today is to use communication not as an adjunct to a strategy and policy, rather utilize the platform to build trust, confidence, self-belief and transparency and "Positioning Communication Perspective". The problem is that the institutional structures that govern the ecosystem thrive on the "Imbalances Related to Resources, Reach, Accountability and Non-Regulation" of the mediums. It is no rocket science when one notices the biased projection of the western media on issues that create ripples on the image, perception and narratives. These structures do not facilitate a fair discourse of narratives rather they suffer from communication distortion due to their mantra of knee jerk communication.

Globally, geostrategic practitioners have suffered the menace of fact checking, in order to ensure fairness and ethics in information management. This unwanted phenomenon has also thrived due to the lack of **"Media literacy"** and awareness amongst people, the inability to critically understand and evaluate content. This phenomenon is one of the biggest push factors ailing the current global information order has led to distortion and lack of understanding of key issues dominating the media space.

In the current global order geostrategic considerations are certainly playing out in the public domain, rather than in hush hushed corridors of power. Policymakers face the challenge of gestures, curated visuals, amplified images, digital tools. Invasion that erases trust, cohesion and transparency in the information ecosystem. Geostrategy, today requires a holistic narrative building exercise wherein traditional and new media format weave together a predictable and comprehensive narrative. It is critical important factor must be to weave and check role and responsibility of AI. Technology driven communication, that does not obliterate transparency and ethics in the domain of strategic messaging. Global consensuses should not fall prey to the wonder tools and algorithms of AI as it would expose the inbuilt fragility of communication through modern tools techniques and content

What the world needs now is a globally accepted fact-checking protocol; a cooperative network of governments, tech platforms, and neutral watchdogs committed to immediate and effective debunking of misinformation. It must be matched with international investments in media literacy initiatives and cross-border transparency frameworks. For in these volatile times, when geopolitics is dictated by optics and perception, the cost of unchecked misinformation is far too high. Strategic communication must be wielded not as a megaphone for chaos, but as a lighthouse of clarity and trust. Because the war for truth is no less important than the war for peace.

The Mantras of Geostrategic Communication in a Hyperconnected World

As we move deeper into the second quarter of the year, the global communication landscape is revealing itself to be one of profound change, disruption, innovation, and ideation. Across continents and platforms, this evolving ecosystem is presenting new challenges to practitioners, analysts, and policymakers in the realms of geopolitics and strategic communication. Audiences around the world are witnessing, often with awe and astonishment, the sheer complexity and diversity that modern communication now entails. The latest phenomenon captivating attention is the AI-generated "Ghibli Effect," a digital trend that reflects a broader transformation in how narratives are produced, consumed, and politicized.

We are increasingly becoming subjects, not just consumers, of algorithms, data interpretation, overbranding, and perhaps, overexposure. This leads us to the moot question: how deep is the impact of such trends and tools on the domain of geostrategic communication? Can aesthetic or digital trends like the Ghibli Effect inform new diplomatic languages, soft power strategies, or even modes of bilateral and multilateral engagement? At first glance, these cultural phenomena might seem disconnected from traditional diplomacy. Yet they hold the potential to reshape the way nations interact, individuals perceive foreign policy, and institutions define global influence.

In today's hyperconnected world, communication is not just a tool for diplomacy—it is diplomacy. The proliferation of real-time information, and the scale at which it is absorbed, has made it increasingly difficult to establish a unified geopolitical narrative. The multiplicity of news streams, each vying to be 'breaking,' creates an environment where reactions become fragmented and short-lived. In such a scenario, formulating a focused communication response becomes almost impossible. Yet, it is now globally recognized that communication is central to policymaking; it cannot remain a peripheral concern in the strategic ecosystem.

One of the critical moments for shaping this narrative could be the upcoming United Nations General Assembly (UNGA), which must consider placing global communication governance on its agenda. A dialogue among global media stakeholders, framed as a "Global Media Roundtable" or "Communication

Assembly," can help dilute aggressive and divisive patterns such as fake news, deepfakes, and synthetic media manipulation. This is not merely a technological issue, it is a diplomatic imperative.

Whether it's strategic alliances like QUAD, BRICS, or forums such as ASEAN or SAARC, there is a growing need to co-create a common communication framework. This is especially vital as generational shifts bring Gen Z and Gen Alpha to the forefront. These digital natives are not just passive recipients of information; they are active producers and influencers of international opinion. Strategic communication must evolve with them in mind.

New ideas and platforms influence the contours of global discourse. The information dissemination process today hinges on the interplay of expertise, experience, and empathy. As communicators race to stay relevant, the ecosystem risks becoming caught up in flair and the excesses of instant communication. In such an environment, the challenge for policymakers and media strategists is to recalibrate the tone and strategy of messaging. It is no longer sufficient to just "speak."

Geostrategic communication is under constant threat from information overload and the infodemic. With every global event instantly translatable into trending hashtags and viral videos, boundaries between statecraft and storytelling are blurring. The rise of visual culture—Instagram reels, AI-generated avatars, TikTok diplomacy—demands that institutions adapt to the speed of sentiment and social perception. Public diplomacy strategies must be reengineered for a world running on 15-second attention spans.

This new terrain demands a fresh narrative infrastructure, one built not just on digital platforms but on shared values and clarity. It is time to reimagine the protocols of narrative building, especially in multilateral settings. There is a dire need to establish common media denominators: shared truths, fact-verification standards, and ethical storytelling principles that guide global information management. These would serve as the backbone of crisis communication, strategic alignment, and de-escalation.

In this moment of flux, traditional media has come under renewed scrutiny. Yet, dismissing it would be a mistake. The legacy model has survived because it is grounded in credibility and long-form comprehension. In contrast to the anonymity of social media, traditional journalism is bound by accountability. Even as we embrace tech-driven formats, the resilience of traditional media and its commitment to deep reporting remain vital. This is especially true in geostrategic communication, which requires nuance and a human-centered approach.

As technologies reshape how nations speak, we must return to fundamentals.

A compelling narrative cannot be built solely through data points and digital graphics. It needs the human voice, the elegance of words, and cultural resonance.

To navigate today's volatile landscape, geostrategic communication must be redefined. We need a shared global framework, cross-generational storytelling, ethical content ecosystems, and renewed faith in traditional media. Above all, diplomacy must remain human-centric. These are not optional, they are essential. In an era where perception shapes reality, the future will belong not to the loudest voices, but to the wisest communicators.

Toward a Global Communication Order: Proposal for an International Communications Committee (ICC)

India's Vision for Regulating Information in the Age of Perception Warfare

Institutions in 2025 are undergoing a cataclysmic shift, driven by changes in perception, geopolitics, multilateral dynamics, and the relentless pursuit of dominance and supremacy. Power shifts today are no longer isolated events. They unfold in a backdrop carefully shaped by design, intent, and deeper strategic purpose, intensified by the rising number of global flashpoints.

Across the board, there's a growing, urgent call to establish a credible institutional framework to manage consistency in geostrategic communication, perception control, and narrative design thinking. As new crises erupt and old conflicts mutate, analysts and observers are increasingly debating the need for a permanent structure, an international body, to oversee the evolving goals of strategic communication, message dissemination, and information architecture.

Despite the frequency and speed with which events now unfold, there are undeniable gaps; gaps in accountability, in alignment between medium, message, and messenger, and in the mechanisms that once held power structures accountable. In the absence of coordination, perception becomes chaos, and messaging becomes a battlefield.

Historically, communication in conflict zones was structured and symbolic, through flags, handwritten messages, trained birds, and direct negotiations. Each breakthrough was a visual hallmark: the hoisting of a white flag, a treaty signed in a formal setting, images carefully curated to reflect truth, resolve, and peace.

The Cold War era saw an expansion in media's role in diplomacy, through carefully orchestrated press conferences, black-and-white footage of summits, and state-controlled messaging that still held narrative power. But the tools were fewer, slower, and traceable.

Fast forward to the present, and communication has exploded into a 24x7, unregulated free-for-all. Social media platforms, podcasts, live videos, and meme culture have blurred the lines between truth, opinion, and fiction. Information itself has become a weapon, with no common watermark of credibility, and no binding global protocol to regulate its use or dissemination.

We are now at a juncture where an International Communications Committee (ICC) is not just desirable, it is essential. This proposed global think tank would comprise representatives from across nations, experts in information warfare, digital ethics, media regulation, and communication law. Its role would be to establish a global framework for communication protocols, fact-verification models, and crisis information standards.

Like the WAVES 2025 Media Summit, which India spearheaded to promote storytelling at the intersection of technology and tradition, the ICC can emerge as a pioneering global institution. India, with its democratic ethos and growing digital influence, is well-positioned to take the lead.

The Preamble and Constitution of the ICC will form its foundational document, rooted in global consensus, aligned with the United Nations Charter and the Sustainable Development Goals (SDGs). It will lay out the moral and strategic compass of the body: to uphold responsible communication, foster global solidarity, and defend truth as a collective value across borders.

The Guiding Principles of the ICC will be simple yet powerful. Communication must be treated as a public good. There should be universal access to verified, factual information, with strong mechanisms of accountability in digital and emerging media spaces. The principles will emphasize respect for national sovereignty, cultural diversity in narrative representation, and a zero-tolerance policy toward misinformation, disinformation, and propaganda warfare.

The Core Functions of the ICC will reflect its commitment to standard-setting and enforcement. A watermark protocol will be developed for all visual media circulated globally, enabling authentication and credibility at the source level. A global fact-check network, powered by artificial intelligence but human-supervised through an independent watchdog, will ensure rapid response to viral misinformation. Emergency dissemination protocols will be designed to standardize and streamline global communication during crises, and the ICC will audit and certify ethical media standards for digital platforms and national outlets alike. The committee will also map, track, and counter the growing arsenal of information warfare tools, ranging from bot networks to deepfakes and manipulated media.

As for Citizens' Participation, the ICC will take a calibrated approach. Citizens will be encouraged to participate as verified digital contributors, trained in ethical journalism and provided with digital identification credentials. The committee will also promote norms for responsible podcasting and content creation. Positive reinforcement mechanisms will be designed to reward those who spread constructive, truthful narratives. While maintaining freedom of expression, the ICC will also recommend clear content standards to ensure platforms reduce the spread of harmful misinformation.

The ICC will also curate Best Practices in Crisis Communication. In moments of war, disaster, or humanitarian strain, the committee will promote storytelling that brings people together, highlighting hope, resilience, and unity. It will also create structures to facilitate narrative exchange between nations, so that lived realities and experiences are humanized rather than politicized. To build institutional readiness, simulation-based training programs will be offered to global media houses, platforms, and content moderators.

On the challenge of Western Media Bias, the ICC will serve as a counterweight to narrative imbalance.

For decades, developing nations have struggled to be seen, heard, and interpreted fairly. The ICC will provide an equitable space for these countries to reclaim narrative agency. It will ensure fair visibility and guard against the politicization of media coverage by dominant geopolitical powers.

To gain traction and credibility, the ICC must begin with a core coalition of aligned countries; India should take the lead as founding convener. This coalition would initiate consultations and regional dialogues modeled on the success of WAVES 2025, creating momentum around the idea of narrative sovereignty. Partnerships must be established with global media alliances, technology platforms, AI ethics councils, and multilateral institutions such as UNESCO, UNDP, and the G20.

Ultimately, the ICC must evolve into a treaty-backed international body, with legal and diplomatic recognition, standard-setting authority, and mechanisms for enforcement. Only then can it meaningfully shape the narrative landscape and restore coherence to the global communication order.

As warfare moves from trenches to timelines, from bullets to bytes, the tools of destruction have become indistinguishable from the tools of communication. This makes the need for a Global Information and Communication Order urgent and inescapable. Through this proposal, India offers the world not just an idea, but a framework, for regulation over chaos, truth over noise, and shared narrative stewardship in times of global flux. The International Communications Committee can be the institution that turns today's informational disorder into tomorrow's collective order.

Let this be the watermark of global trust, visible, traceable, and built to last.

Film Festivals and the 3C Mantra: Creativity, Culture, Commerce

The 3C's mantra that defines the film festival ecosystem: Creativity, Culture, and Commerce, has become the cornerstone of a global cinematic renaissance. Today, film festivals are not just glamorous red-carpet affairs or celebrity-driven events. They are transformative platforms unlocking new opportunities for content creation, cross-cultural collaboration, global networking, strategic partnerships, and narrative innovation. In short, they are the modern-day crucibles where storytelling meets strategy.

From Cannes to Berlin, Venice to IFFI, Locarno to Sundance, film festivals have evolved into sophisticated arenas that redefine cinematic expression. They are reshaping the celluloid experience through experiential storytelling, sustainable creative roadmaps, and tech-enabled narratives that resonate across boundaries. Their evolution reflects a collective aspiration to reimagine the medium, not just in how films are made, but in how they are shared, discussed, and remembered.

The world's most celebrated film festivals have retained their traditional flavor while courageously stepping into new territory. The Cannes Film Festival, for instance, remains a symbol of glamour, yet now actively promotes ecological awareness and inclusivity through programs like the "Cinema for the Climate" section. Similarly, the Venice Biennale embraces innovation through its Virtual Reality section, while TIFF (Toronto International Film Festival) has become known for elevating social-issue films into the awards circuit. These examples highlight how the 3C's are no longer abstract ideals, they are tangible, operational principles shaping programming and policy.

The unified objective is clear: visualize the future of cinema through the lens of commercial viability, cutting-edge technology, and artistic innovation. And festivals, in balancing these objectives, are becoming incubators of excellence, where ideas are born, refined, and launched into the world.

Film markets are an integral part of this new cinematic landscape. Events such as Marché du Film at Cannes and Film Bazaar at IFFI serve as value-creation platforms where creativity meets investment. These markets offer a single-window ecosystem for distributors, producers, and emerging talent to forge deals, secure financing, and explore global collaborations.

Today's commercial landscape at festivals is populated by accredited agents, pavilions, exhibitors, and stakeholders who are not just selling films; they're shaping the business of storytelling. Co-production deals, project financing, distribution arrangements, and IP partnerships are negotiated in these spaces, affirming the financial architecture of the festival ecosystem. Notably, the commercial value of festivals is no longer transactional but transformational. They're redefining how cinema is monetized and how stories are positioned globally. And in the age of OTT, film festivals have also become spaces for digital content negotiations, IP marketing, and branded storytelling ventures.

Each global festival has carved a distinct identity. While Cannes stands for glamour and auteur prestige, Berlinale champions political cinema, and

Locarno thrives on experimentation. These brands have emerged from consistent visual language, storytelling themes, fashion statements, and strategic stakeholder engagement.

In this ecosystem, branding is not just about logos or campaigns, it's about shaping a cinematic culture. It's the deliberate interplay of Creativity, Culture, Content, and Consistency, the 4C's of festival branding. The buzz, the arc lights, the curated installations, and even the architectural design of venues contribute to the festival's emotional and cultural memory.

India's growing role in the global cinematic discourse is exemplified by the Bharat Pavilion at Cannes, designed by the National Institute of Design, Ahmedabad. Titled *The Sutradhara*, or storyteller, it reflects India's fusion of tradition and innovation. With its 2024 theme, *Create in India*, the Pavilion spotlighted India's vibrant cinematic heritage, technological readiness, and openness to global partnerships.

More than just a national representation, the Bharat Pavilion has become a diplomatic and cultural bridge; connecting India's storytellers with producers, buyers, critics, and policymakers from across the world. It's a space where artistry meets policy, and where culture is leveraged for creative diplomacy. The Bharat Parv, an integral part of the Pavilion experience, adds further dimension to celebrating Indian cuisine, music, craftsmanship, and diversity. This new format of global storytelling mirrors the idea of *Vasudhaiva Kutumbakam*: the world as one family. And importantly, it sends a clear message: India is not just a content provider, it's a creative force and co-production hub.

Film festivals today function as living ecosystems: nurturing voices, encouraging risk-taking, and building transnational communities. Their role in shaping public perception, fostering policy discourse, and enabling commercial success is more relevant than ever. Whether it's Cannes' "Cinema for the Climate," Venice's Virtual Reality section, or IFFI's mainstream-indie convergence, the new festival circuit is breaking boundaries with purpose. It's showcasing new cinematic languages, driven by talent, diversity, and digital disruption.

As the film festival landscape continues to evolve, the 3C's—Creativity, Culture, and Commerce—remain the North Star. With countries like India building immersive, multi-stakeholder pavilions and enabling co-creation through policy and soft power, the red carpet is no longer just about glitz. It's about vision, value, and voice, and who gets to tell the next global story. Beyond the flashbulbs and premieres, cinema is being reimagined; as a force for diplomacy, opportunity, and global connection. Storytelling now transcends screens; it lives in pavilions, platforms, and policies. Film festivals are no longer just stages, they're statements. And those who wield narrative, innovation, and collaboration won't just watch the future unfold, they'll script it.

The evolution of music consumption: From soulful rituals to scrolling reels

There's a peculiar kind of magic that only music holds, a force that reaches into the deepest corners of the human soul, bridges generations and quietly scores the background of revolutions, romances and rainy evenings. For the longest time, music wasn't just something we played, it was something we lived. It was the sitar humming through a quiet evening, the grainy texture of a vinyl crackling to life or a voice trembling with truth that could shake you to your core.

Music was ritual, rebellion and revelation all rolled into one.

A very important musical milestone in our life was the commencement of All India Radio's Vividh Bharti. Vividh Bharati was not just a station. It was a presence.

Mornings would be graced by Saigal's songs echoing in the house. Programmes like Purani Filmon Ka Sangeet would be a portal to an era of elegant music and timeless classics by the iconic Lata Mangeshkar, Mukesh and others.

Bhoole Bisre Geet was a dedicated programme for discovering melodies that had fallen through time's cracks. Man Chahey Geet gave listeners the opportunity to request for songs to be played.

Today, in a world where a single swipe can summon a thousand songs, it's easy to forget the weight that a melody once carried. The way we consume music has changed, and with that, so have our rituals, our preferences, and even what it means to truly listen.

For many of us growing up in the 80s and 90s, music wasn't available on demand. It had to be found, earned and cherished. The radio, especially All India Radio's Yuva Vani, was a lifeline to a world that felt just beyond reach. That crackly broadcast might be your first brush with the Bee Gees, The Carpenters or The Beatles. And if you really liked something, you made the pilgrimage to the nearest music store. The cassettes there weren't just tapes, they were time capsules, treasures to be guarded, rewound and replayed till the ribbon wore thin. The secret love letters. Sharing music meant sharing a part of yourself.

Then came the 90s, and with it, an evolution of cool. Entered MTV, Channel

V and VHI, portals to global soundscapes that brought hip-hop, rap, grunge and glossy pop into Indian homes. These weren't just music channels, they were curators of identity. If you revolution gave people choice. For the first time, music wasn't just what your parents played at Sunday brunch, it was yours. The Walkman became your most prized possession.

Car stereos turned traffic jams into private concerts. Mixtapes were passed around like RETRO MIX VOL 2

If you weren't listening to Madonna, Michael Jackson or Alanis Moris-sette, you weren't really in the loop. Music videos became mini blockbusters. Lyrics changed. So did language. Your music taste became a marker of who you were or who you wanted to be.

And yet, even then, discovery was a journey. Music was a friend, a guide, a mirror.

Fast forward to now, and that relationship looks entirely differ-ent. Ask a Gen Z or Gen Alpha kid where they discover music, and the answer is instant: Instagram Reels, YouTube Shorts and sometimes TikTok. We've moved from full-length albums to 15-second hooks, from cover art to choreography.

The experience is now algorithm-driven, hyper-visual and tailored for virality.

Today, the beat has to drop in the first three sec-onds. A hook step can make a song explode. Platforms reward engagement, not always emotion.

Reels can amplify a chorus to millions, but sometimes strip away the slow burn of a full track.

Music is more accessible, sure, but it can also feel disposable. Yet, in this scroll-and-skip world, something beautiful still happens.

Korean pop track can go viral in Delhi. K-pop Fandoms, arguably the most powerful modern music communi-ties, have redefined loyalty. love and language barriers. A Blackpink teaser can set off more excitement than some film trail-ers. Korean producers and choreographers have inspired not just global dance moves, but global feels. Music today is less about borders and more about belonging. Closer home.

Artists like Rishabh Rikhiram Sharma, a young sitar virtuoso, are proof that the past and future can coexist. His Instagram and YouTube videos blending classical ragas with lo-fi beats are both rooted and futuristic. He's not just keeping the sitar alive; he's making it relevant for a generation raised on memes and music apps. Through creators like him, traditional Indian instruments are finding new resonance and relevance on digital stages.

But let's be honest, the nostalgia still lingers. There's something irreplaceable about waiting for your favorite song to come on the radio or pressing "record" at just the right time to catch it. There was intimacy in that anticipation. A tactile joy in unwrapping a new cassette.A sense of communion in sitting with someone, quietly sharing a song. That depth, of listening and of being present, is what many feel we're losing. Music used to stop the world. Now it often just plays in the background of it.

Still, perhaps every generation finds its own magic. And maybe, despite the tech and the trends. we're all after the same thing: that moment when music just gets you.

When a verse finds your wound before you do. When a beat matches your heartbeat. When a line makes you feel seen.

Today, though, music lovers often find themselves in a quiet catch-22 torn between admiring the precision of AI-composed tracks and yearning for the raw imperfection of natural sounds and handmade instruments. The soul still seeks resonance, but the source feels blurred.

So whether you're scrolling through Reels or rewinding a tape, remember this: the platforms may change, but music's purpose does-n't. It's still here to move us, to connect us, to remind us of who we are and who we can be.

After all, isn't that what being a listener is really about?

Communicating Geostrategy: Why Narratives Matter More Than Maps

When we talk about global power today, we rarely talk just about weapons or borders anymore, we talk about stories. We talk about who controls the narrative. That's essentially what geostrategic communication is: shaping how a country is perceived in the global mindspace, and making that perception work in its favour.

But this isn't some new-age buzzword. Geopolitical communication has always been around, it's just evolved with time. Earlier, it meant states issuing statements through newspapers or prime ministers addressing the nation on the radio. Think World War II–era propaganda, or Cold War shortwave radio stations like Voice of America and Radio Moscow. Back then, it was all about control. One nation. One narrative. One channel.

And honestly, it worked. Radio, in particular, was a game-changer. It crossed borders, bypassed censorship, and reached straight into homes. Even today, in certain conflict zones and remote regions, radio remains strangely relevant, mostly because it doesn't need literacy, internet, or high bandwidth. But its influence? Fading. Because the world doesn't just consume information anymore, we engage with it.

Enter the era of podcasts, YouTube diplomacy, Twitter handles run by embassies, and viral reels of prime ministers hugging kids. Communication is no longer just press releases and speeches, it's aesthetics, relatability, and digital fluency.

Take podcasts, for instance. They offer depth, analysis, and storytelling in ways older mediums never could. But here's the catch, they assume a certain level of media literacy. If you don't know how to separate opinion from fact, or narrative from manipulation, they can mislead as easily as they inform. And in large parts of the Global South, where digital literacy is still uneven, this becomes a serious barrier.

That's the paradox: newer mediums are more powerful, but not always more accessible. Unlike radio, which needed only a working device and a signal, digital media assumes a lot, stable internet, tech access, and an ability to process and filter information in a cluttered, fast-paced environment.

And even when digital access exists, cultural context matters. A podcast that resonates with college students in Boston might fall flat in Bengaluru or Bujumbura. Tone, language, trust, and platform choice all play a role in whether or not the message lands.

The biggest change? Earlier, states used to *talk at* people. Now they're expected to *talk with* them. That's a massive shift in power. Citizens are no longer passive recipients. They respond, they critique, they shape public opinion. So governments can't just rely on official statements or dry diplomacy anymore, they need Instagram stories, humour, memes, sometimes even influencers to get the message across.

And it's not just citizens watching. It's the whole world. One misstep goes viral in minutes. One well-timed speech can win soft power points overnight. Every move is under scrutiny, every silence too.

Even international aid, development partnerships, or university collaborations are being seen as extensions of diplomatic storytelling. Countries are now curating not just what they do, but how they're seen doing it. Perception, in this climate, is often more powerful than fact.

There's a growing understanding that you can't talk about global influence without including young people, technology, and culture. They're not just the future, they're the present. And they're also the most at-risk group when it comes to misinformation, online manipulation, and polarising narratives.

That's why building *media literacy*, and not just access, is critical. If we want our youth to be global citizens who can engage with geopolitics meaningfully, they need to be trained to ask: Who is saying this? Why are they saying it? What's missing?

Diplomacy today isn't just about closed-door negotiations. It's about what a country posts, what it promotes, and how it responds to criticism. It's about the influencers it supports, the films it exports, the causes it stands for, and even how its leaders dress and speak in international forums. In a way, everything is strategy now.

This is where soft power meets strategic intention. Whether it's India promoting Ayurveda and yoga on global stages, Korea exporting K-pop and K-dramas, or the U.S. amplifying democratic values through entertainment and tech, these are not coincidences. These are *deliberate communications*, dressed as culture.

We need countries, especially in the Global South, to invest in strategic communication, not just infrastructure. To train their diplomats, bureaucrats, and youth in the language of influence. To create spaces where conversation replaces propaganda. To build digital muscle that can counter disinformation without becoming censorship. And above all, to tell stories that are true, compelling, and rooted in values people can relate to.

We need communication modules embedded in schools and colleges that don't just teach "media studies" but prepare students to be defenders of truth and decoders of complexity. We need public campaigns that promote *listening*, not just speaking louder. And we need local storytellers empowered to tell national stories from ground-up, not top-down.

Geostrategic communication is, at its heart, storytelling with intent. And like all good stories, it requires authenticity, resonance, and relevance. It must evolve with its audience, be it through a dusty transistor in rural Bihar or a Spotify podcast in Boston. As nations compete not just for territory but for trust, attention, and belief, the future of geopolitics will belong to those who can tell the best story, and make it stick.

Because in today's world, power isn't just about who has the biggest army or

GDP. It's about who controls the narrative, and who knows how to listen, shape, and speak with clarity in a world of noise.

And if we're smart, we'll teach the next generation not just to scroll, but to see. Not just to repost, but to understand. Because the next war might not be fought on land, but on timelines.

India's Quiet Revolution: How Yoga Redefined Global Power

In a world constantly jostling for attention, through missiles, money, and media, India has managed to slip something quietly into the global bloodstream: yoga. Not just the stretch-on-a-mat version that floods Instagram, but the real thing, an ancient, rooted philosophy that has slowly become one of the most persuasive tools of soft power diplomacy in the 21st century. It's not flashy, it doesn't demand loyalty, but it lingers; and that's where its magic lies.

For the past 10 years, yoga's rise has been deliberate, strategic, and honestly, quite beautiful to watch. The turning point came in 2014, when Prime Minister Narendra Modi proposed the idea of an International Day of Yoga at the United Nations. 177 countries backed it, not because they wanted to do India a favor, but because yoga had already embedded itself in their societies. That was the win, not just the declaration itself, but the global readiness to accept that this was more than India's past; it was part of humanity's future. Since then, June 21 has transformed from a cultural celebration into something much deeper, a show of presence, not power; of balance, not bluster.

And that's what makes yoga such an exceptional soft power tool. It doesn't yell, it invites. It doesn't push a product; it offers a practice. While other cultural exports often come dressed in capitalism or carry subtle imperial agendas, yoga feels clean, disarming even. Its strength lies in its quietness. From New York to Nairobi, Tokyo to Toronto, the sight of thousands moving together in breath and stillness is not just aesthetic, it's symbolic. In a time where nations scream over each other, yoga listens, and people respond.

Back home, the Ministry of Ayush has played a crucial role in deepening this influence. From local wellness programs and school modules to international MOUs and yoga certification frameworks, the past two decades have seen a real, measurable investment in making yoga accessible, authentic, and global. This isn't just branding, it's cultural stewardship, and it matters. Because when a country not only preserves but exports its deepest values, and does so with humility, it earns something far more valuable than visibility; it earns trust.

This year, the International Day of Yoga 2025 campaign is themed *"Yoga for One Earth, One Health"*—a line that captures, in five words, everything the world is craving: connection, sustainability, healing. After years of pandemic panic, mental health breakdowns, and climate anxiety, the idea that the health of our bodies is directly tied to the health of our planet doesn't feel like a philosophy anymore; it feels like a necessity. Ayush's campaigns this year reflect that urgency. Over 30,000 organizations are joining the 'Yoga Sangam', turning parks, schoolyards, hospitals, and railway platforms into yoga grounds. These aren't token events; they're public declarations that India's contribution to global peace and wellbeing will not be transactional, it will be transformative.

And then there's *YogAndhra 2025*, one of the most ambitious state campaigns we've seen in years. Two crore people, a month-long activation, a mass event along the Visakhapatnam coastline—it's massive, and honestly, deeply moving. Not because of the numbers, but because of what they represent: ordinary people coming together, voluntarily, in a moment of pause. That's the real diplomacy, not the flags, not the official handshakes. Just breath, stillness, surrender; and in that shared silence, India speaks louder than any press release ever could.

What makes all of this even more powerful is the tenor of yoga itself. It's not ornamental, it's foundational. Yoga doesn't demand performance, it demands presence. And in a hyper-digitized, algorithm-driven world, that's revolutionary. Yoga has no nation, but it does have an origin; and every time someone anywhere rolls out a mat and begins their practice, they are, whether they know it or not, engaging with India, not politically, but spiritually and philosophically. That's legacy; and that's how soft power actually works.

Health diplomacy is another layer in this story that often gets overlooked. In a time when the world is buckling under non-communicable diseases, burnout, and post-pandemic trauma, India's offering isn't just ancient, it's relevant. Yoga is preventive, sustainable; it teaches you to listen to your body, manage your mind, and regulate your breath. That's public health without a prescription. It's affordable, scalable, and deeply human. The fact that international bodies like the WHO are now aligning with Ayush to explore integrative health models is no coincidence; it's recognition.

But to fully understand yoga's impact, you have to go beyond the policy speak. Yoga isn't about flexibility; it's about balance. It's not about how you look, it's about how you feel. It doesn't sell transformation in 21 days; it teaches you to surrender to slow, patient evolution. When someone in Buenos Aires or Berlin or Bengaluru sits in silence, they're not just accessing a wellness tool; they're entering a cultural portal, one that leads, always, back to India.

And that's what makes yoga such a rare diplomatic asset. It doesn't just generate influence; it generates affection. It's not transactional. It's not about lobbying. It's about resonance, and resonance lasts. India, through yoga, is not trying to dominate global narratives. It's anchoring them, centering them, reminding the world that wellness, at its core, is not a luxury; it's a right. And that stillness, in a fractured, frantic world, is not weakness; it's power.

So as India gears up for another powerful edition of IDY, it's not just about the scale of participation or the number of countries involved. It's about what yoga continues to signify: that even in a global order shaped by conflict, chaos, and competition, there is space, sacred, silent, strong; for something slower, deeper, and more human. Yoga isn't just India's cultural gift; it's its geopolitical signature. Not loud, but lasting.

And maybe that's the whole point. In a world obsessed with speed and spectacle, yoga reminds us that the real revolution begins when we learn to just stop, breathe, and listen; to ourselves, and to each other.

The New Soft Power Mantra: How India is Rewriting Global Influence

Challenges, experiences, opportunities, and imagination have shaped the India story in the soft power terrain over the last 11 years of the Modi government since 2014. In this period, soft power has not only emerged as a guiding force, it has become the soul of India's diplomatic strategy, propelling the country to new heights and redefining the parameters of global knowledge exchange.

The term *soft power*, coined by Harvard professor Joseph Nye in the 1980s, originally referred to a country's ability to shape the preferences of others through appeal and attraction, rather than coercion or force. While Nye focused largely on American cultural exports and value systems, India's approach to soft power has been more layered, rooted in its civilizational depth, democratic ethos, and an inclusive, pluralistic vision of global engagement.

Over the past decade, India has redefined this term through distinctly indigenous lenses. The collation, collaboration, and curation of new ideas, themes, and platforms have reshaped how we understand and apply soft power. From yoga and Ayurveda to cinema, cuisine, education, and digital infrastructure, India has offered a fresh 'cuisine of thought', blending tradition with modernity. These exports are not just cultural; they are connectors, linking India with people, policies, and perceptions across geographies.

India's pride of place in the global soft power discourse today is no accident. It is the result of strategic clarity, cultural confidence, and a reimagined diplomatic approach grounded in lived culture rather than formal posturing. Prime Minister Narendra Modi's leadership has given soft power a renewed focus, anchored in participatory energy, collaboration, and innovation. What has emerged is a people-first soft power matrix, lived through festivals, amplified in films, and echoed across student exchanges, diaspora engagement, and tech-enabled global outreach.

This philosophy was most vividly on display during India's G20 Presidency in 2023. The theme, *Vasudhaiva Kutumbakam*: "One Earth, One Family, One Future", was more than symbolic. It became a lived experience. Music, crafts, cuisine, and digital storytelling were seamlessly interwoven into the diplomatic fabric of the summit. Leaders didn't just engage in dialogue; they immersed themselves in India's diversity, art, and cultural vibrancy. By transforming policy platforms into cultural showcases, India introduced a new grammar of influence, one that communicates as much through symbolism as through strategy. It demonstrated clearly that India doesn't divide tradition from innovation, it weaves them together.

This year's International Day of Yoga, celebrated globally on 21st June 2025, further amplified that spirit with the theme *"Yoga for One Earth, One Health."* It was a powerful articulation of India's timeless belief in personal well-being as the cornerstone of collective harmony. From the UN headquarters to ancient temple backdrops and bustling city squares across continents, the celebration reaffirmed yoga's role as a cornerstone of India's soft power story. Indian missions across the globe led these events with grace and purpose, reaffirming that India's influence is felt through peace, not power.

A critical pillar in India's soft power evolution has been education diplomacy. Prime Minister Modi has consistently championed the potential of education tourism as a global connector. Initiatives like *Study in India*, the growing network of Institutes of Eminence, and expanding academic collaborations with foreign universities reflect India's ambition to become a global education hub, not just for affordability, but for its unique blend of ancient wisdom and forward-thinking pedagogy.

The National Education Policy (NEP) 2020 has been a turning point in this journey. With its emphasis on multilingualism, critical thinking, and global academic integration, NEP 2020 is positioning India as a destination for both substance and spirit. India today is not just offering degrees; it is offering a philosophy. Platforms like DIKSHA, designed for digital, inclusive learning, are now being studied by countries seeking low-cost, scalable educational models that democratize access and encourage lifelong learning.

Indian cinema has long been a cultural export, but in the past few years, it has evolved into a powerful soft power weapon. From Payal Kapadia's historic win at Cannes 2024 to the worldwide resonance of South Indian films, Indian storytelling has pushed through linguistic, geographic, and thematic boundaries. These films are more than entertainment; they are emotional emissaries, carrying Indian values, visuals, and voices into hearts across the globe.

Alongside cinema, India's Digital Public Infrastructure (DPI), comprising platforms like UPI, Aadhaar, and DigiLocker, has transformed the country into a model for ethical, people-centric technology. This is soft power with utility, digital tools that serve public good and offer replicable frameworks for emerging economies. India is no longer just exporting culture; it is exporting scalable, inclusive systems.

India's 32 million–strong diaspora continues to be a potent force in this soft power matrix. Their contributions across sectors, from politics and business to science and arts, position India as a truly global node. Initiatives like Pravasi Bharatiya Divas and sustained engagement with youth of Indian origin have ensured that the diaspora remains deeply connected, not just nostalgically but functionally.

At the same time, India's democratic resilience, its electoral strength, media pluralism, and civic vibrancy, continues to be its most enduring moral soft power. In a global climate fraught with polarization and digital disinformation, India's messy but vibrant democracy remains a beacon of balance and endurance.

The last 11 years have not merely expanded India's soft power toolkit; they have reimagined the entire arena. Soft power today is not a side narrative; it is central to how India sees itself and projects itself. It flows through food, faith, fintech, festivals, and films. It educates through NEP, heals through Ayurveda, and connects through yoga. It does not lecture, it lives. It does not dominate, it draws. India's greatest strength lies in its ability to blend civilization with innovation, emotion with execution. Its soft power is not ornamental; it is operational. Not passive, but persuasive. And in a world increasingly divided by noise, India is offering a voice rooted in harmony.

The future of influence may be digital, mobile, and global, but it is also deeply Indian. And now more than ever, the world is listening.

Tourism as a transformational force

There was a time when travel was all about checking boxes of how many places you could squeeze into an itinerary, or how many pictures you could take in front of famous monuments.

There was a time when travel was all about checking boxes of how many places you could squeeze into an itinerary, or how many pictures you could take in front of famous monuments. But that's changed. Travel today is about something else entirely. It's about what the journey does to you.

And in that quiet, powerful shift, India is finding its moment. This isn't just a country you visit. This is a country that stays with you .

India isn't trying to compete with the world on spectacle because it doesn't have to. What it offers is something much harder to find: depth, soul and meaning. And that's exactly what more and more travellers seem to be looking for. From someone recovering in a hospital bed in Kerala to a young student arriving for a semester in Delhi, from a pilgrim lighting a diya by the Ganga to a filmmaker capturing a sunrise in Sikkim, India is shaping stories, not just vacations. The numbers reflect this intent. In the Union Budget 2025–26, the government set aside Rs 2541.06 crore for tourism a strong, clear message that this sector isn't just about revenue anymore.

It's about identity. It's about how we present ourselves to the world, how we open our doors not just to guests, but to fellow seekers. Prime Minister Narendra

Modi summed it up in a way that really stayed with me: "Tourism in India is not just about sightseeing. It is about discovering the soul of a nation." And you can feel that shift, especially in education tourism. There's something beautiful about how India long known for its wisdom, its philosophy and its thinkers is now rediscovering its roots as a global classroom. Yes, the Study in India initiative is making it easier for students from other countries to come here, but it's more than a policy.

It's a feeling. In our classrooms, students don't just gain knowledge; they experience a culture that's messy, layered and alive. They learn from teachers, yes, but also from street conversations, temple chants, shared meals, latenight debates. There's no single way to learn in India. And maybe that's what makes it unforgettable. Then there's healing. Not the kind that begins and ends with prescriptions, but the kind that holds your hand through the entire process. India's emergence as a medical tourism destination is no accident. People from all over the world are coming here for treatments that might cost them a lifetime's savings elsewhere. But they stay for something far more profound – the warmth, the gentleness and the unspoken comfort that comes when care feels personal. Our doctors may use cutting-edge machines, but they still take the time to ask how you're feeling beyond the reports. And sometimes that's what makes all the difference.

Healing, here, doesn't just fix. It transforms. And in a world, that's constantly noisy, constantly rushing, India continues to offer silence. Not the absence of sound, but the kind of stillness that lets you hear yourself again. Spiritual tourism isn't a marketing term here, it's something woven into the air. It's in the way people lower their voices as they walk into a shrine. It's in the eyes of a monk in a Ladakh monastery. It's in the bells that ring at dusk in a small-town temple. For many, it's their first real pause in years. A place where nobody asks who you are, only how you feel. And that simplicity can be life-changing. And then, unexpectedly, there's film. The kind of cinema that takes you somewhere else, even when you're sitting in your living room.

India has always had the landscapes, the architecture, and the drama – but now it has a system that welcomes global filmmakers too. With easier permissions, incentives, and infrastructure, more films are being made here, and every film becomes a window, a visual love letter to the places we call home. As the Prime Minister once said, "Cinema brings people to India before they even land here." It's true. For so many people abroad, their first glimpse of India is through a scene, an emotion on screen that stays with them long after the credits roll. What makes all of this meaningful is that it's not being left to chance. The government's plan to develop 50 world-class tourist destinations is rooted in real vision. These aren't going to be just polished-up spots for sightseeing.

These are spaces designed for change for memorymaking, for learning, for healing, for belonging. They'll hold stories of visitors who came for one thing, and left with something they couldn't have imagined. As India moves toward 2047, its 100th year of independence, tourism is no longer on the side line. It's becoming a central part of how we imagine ourselves in the world. And honestly, it's fitting. Because this country has always been about journeys. Not just the ones you take on the road, but the ones that change the way you see, think, feel, and live. This is the new India. It isn't asking the world to come and take a tour. It's asking the world to come and find a part of itself here. And that invitation feels both old and new, rooted in our past, but wide open to the future. And maybe that's why it's working.

India's creative ambition has swept the world

India's Media and Entertainment (M&E) sector is standing at the cusp of remarkable innovation, transformation, creativity and quest for being the global content hub.

India's Media and Entertainment (M&E) sector is standing at the cusp of remarkable innovation, transformation, creativity and quest for being the global content hub. What was once a conventional industry is now a pulsating creative force, where traditional storytelling merges with cutting-edge technology, and content creators are quietly and consistently pushing the boundaries of what digital entrepreneurship can look like.

This isn't just about numbers or growth charts anymore, it's about shaping culture, inspiring movements, and placing India firmly on the global creative map. Welcome to India's M&E sector, a sprawling canvas we're filling with vibrant orange hues, one bold stroke at a time. We've stepped into what economists now call the Orange Economy, a creative economy rooted in intellectual property, culture, and innovation. And in India's case, this isn't theory, it's being lived every day. Whether it's a film shoot in Ramoji, a gaming studio in Bangalore, a web series in Delhi, or a podcast in someone's bedroom in Lucknow, this economy spans every shade of creativity and expression.

The shift is clear; creativity isn't just celebrated, it's finally being counted as economic capital. What began as baby steps eleven years ago, has culminated in a giant leap that has transformed the Media and Entertainment ecosystem 360° with focus on harnessing India's potential as a creator of rich content, cross-cultural dialogue, knowledge and storytelling within this ecosystem At the WAVES 2025 summit, Prime Minister Modi laid it out with clarity; India isn't here to play catchup. The theme, "Connecting Creators," wasn't just a line, it was a declaration. We are looking at a future where collaboration, across platforms, formats, and even countries, is the heartbeat of progress.

And the data? It's not just promising, it's staggering. According to EY, India's creator economy is growing at a compound annual growth rate of 18 per cent. From Rs 19 billion in 2023, we're heading toward Rs 34 billion by 2026. But beyond the numbers lies something more vital, the proof that India's creative backbone is getting stronger, bolder, and more indispensable to the larger economic narrative. By 2028, India is set to become the third-largest M&E market in the world. Let that sink in. We're no longer a satellite orbiting global culture; we're becoming one of its primary sources. That shift is visible everywhere: in the deals being signed, the global remakes of Indian IPs, the Oscar shortlists, and in the cultural fluency with which Indian stories are now received.

We're living in a moment where Indian content flows across borders faster than a meme. Geography and language are no longer barriers; they're launchpads. Whether it's a Tamil thriller trending in Tokyo or a Punjabi track tearing through charts in Toronto, one thing's clear: our stories are being heard, seen, and felt. And no, they don't need translation, but subtitles help. The beauty of India's M&E sector today lies in its multi-dimensional value. It informs, through news, educational content, and civic platforms. It entertains, through immersive films, short reels, and expansive gaming worlds. It sells, by blending content with commerce in ways that feel seamless.

And it builds, by giving people platforms to express themselves, grow professionally, and turn creativity into livelihood. That's the magic of this moment. Creation and consumption are both democratized. A 15-second reel can spark conversations; a Twitter thread can reshape public opinion. You can go from scrolling to storytelling in seconds. The lines have blurred, in the best way possible. And while audiences are hungrier than ever for fresh, authentic content, the real gamechanger has been technology. New revenue streams are emerging by the minute, from virtual reality shows to AI-generated music, blockchainbacked ownership of content, and participatory storytelling that lets the viewer shape the plot.

What felt like science fiction five years ago is now just another day at the M&E office. This sector is no longer about delivering content, it's about delivering experiences. Think unified search tools across OTTs, seamless logins, subscription management, and personalized recommendations so sharp they know you better than you know yourself. These aren't just tools; they're the future of audience loyalty. Over the past eleven years, evolution has been nothing short of a metamorphosis. We've moved from linear, one-way broadcasting to a dynamic, two-way ecosystem of storytelling, discovery, and emotional connection. Today's M&E sector is not just a marketplace; it's a movement that has been given the push of "Vasudhaiva Kutumbakam" by the Prime Minister.

We are witnessing a "Jugalbandi" of themes, ideas coupled with new approaches and strategies. And if there's one way to frame this transformation, it's through the 4 Vs: Vision, Value, Voice, and Variety. Together, they've created a foundation where M&E isn't just a sector; it's a statement. Of intent, of identity, of

India's global creative ambition. We're at a point now where opportunities are overflowing. There's space for consolidation, fresh formats, new partnerships, and business models we haven't even imagined yet. Whether you're a legacy broadcaster or a lone content creator, there's a seat at the table. Because this isn't just an industry; it's a revolution.

Call it what you will, a cultural moment, a creative uprising, or simply a sector on steroids. But one thing's for sure: the M&E space has become a Mahakumbh of ideas. Everyone's converging, techies, artists, marketers, musicians, animators, producers, dreamers. And what's coming out of that confluence? Something bold, something original, something unmistakably Indian. As India walks, runs, and sometimes sprints toward becoming a global entertainment superpower, one truth emerges above all: the orange economy is not just a metaphor anymore. It's real, it's roaring, and it's redefining not just how the world sees Indian creativity, but how Indian creativity sees the world.

Revisiting a legend

In the day and age of instant communication, where content and public memory is short, swift and fleeting, acknowledgement of icons and celebrating their centenary is always a special moment. A centenary celebration is not just rewinding into the past, it is a memory jog spanning over hundred years to revisit the rich legacy of icons, who were not just individuals but craftsmen of innovation and excellence. The birth centenary of Guru Dutt, one of India's most brilliant film personalities, falls on 9 July.

It is an occasion to dive deep into his style, expression, perception and creativity spanning several decades. Guru Dutt was much ahead of his times; his centenary reminds us of his genius and his contribution to Hindi cinema. The Guru Dutt era reminds us of our classic and cinematic roots. His perspective on cinema has given us a meaningful relationship to bridge generations through art, creativity and simple storytelling. His era reiterated the transformative power of cinema, giving audiences an unprecedented experience of emotion, artistry and living reality.

As a creative artist, Guru Dutt's career ended tragically at a relatively young age, and the cinema world lost one of its most expressive film makers, whose work explored human sentiments in an "uncharacteristic style". Guru Dutt gave the "black and white era of celluloid" new themes and cinematic techniques that redefined the art of film-making. The beauty of Guru Dutt's movies was his method of engagement with audiences, who were introduced to a new form of creative passion, cinematic exploration and complex yet realistic symbolism. Guru Dutt in all his films placed the power of "silent emotion and expression" as the centre-piece of his style of storytelling.

As a film maker he handled complex human situation through the lens of experimentation that wove in idealism, turmoil, distress and suffering, projected through the characters of every film. His range of creativity was truly unlimited. His bouquet of films offered and navigated a variety of themes, situations, unique cinematic situations, style and language. Pyaasa, his masterpiece and magnum opus, is truly a masterclass for viewing and understanding the complexity of human life through tragic situations, deceit, alienation and quest for perfection. Pyaasa placed Guru Dutt in a different league giving him international acclaim and acknowledgement in his pursuit of cinema.

Guru Dutt combined artistic philosophy with his practical moods, methods and ideas. Kaagaz Ke Phool (1959), though a box office failure, had a cinematic grandeur, challenging themes and melodious music, giving it a unique visual identity. Critics still wonder why this master piece failed. Were melancholy and pain overstretched, and thus rejected by audiences at the box office? The lack of fulfilling dreams and aspirations remained a critical cog in Guru Dutt's creative template. Music was the lifeline of Guru Dutt's repertoire. His musical jugalbandi in several of his films showcased the power of shabd, swar and sangeet, a unique jugalbandi, which gave tunes and melodies that his fans remember even today. His films Aar Par, Pyaasa, Chaudhvin Ka Chand and Kagaz ke Phool portrayed songs with intricate lyrics, choreography, an emotional narrative and a soulful rendition.

The songs in his movies were a part of an emotional journey in search of hope, optimism and at times portraying disillusionment. For example Pyaasa's songs reflected the inner conflict and turmoil of a human, the contradictions of life. Guru Dutt had a unique sixth sense for music. He always visualised storytelling through poetry and melodies. His songs though a part of the entertainment grid, reflected the psychological rhythm of his characters. Songs in his movies had a deeper meaning portraying a reality check and critique of human life and situations. His partnership with Sahir Ludhianvi has given us immortal gems. Who does not understand the relevance of "Yeh Duniya Agar Mil Bhi Jaye to Kya hai". Camera work was Guru Dutt's brahamastra. The camera movement and placement in his films gave audiences a peek into his thought process.

Each shot was carefully processed, placed and positioned. Each frame showcased the power of emotion, expression and interface. We often wonder that if social media had existed in Guru Dutt's time would his underrated masterpiece Kaagaz Ke Phool have received the greater recognition he so truly deserved? The truth is Guru Dutt's cinema was not made for virality. It was made for those willing to sit with discomfort, to find poetry in pain, and to witness beauty in brokenness. His stories were slow-burning laments of a society in transition, and in their stillness lay their strength. Perhaps the noise of social media might have drowned that subtlety.

And yet, perhaps his soulstirring visuals and timeless themes would have found new life online, inspiring a new generation to look beyond the obvious.

Did he receive the recognition he truly deserved? Not in his time. His genius was too nuanced, too ahead of its era. But art like his doesn't fade, it waits. And today, we revisit his films with reverence, almost as if making up for the past's oversight. Guru Dutt's legacy stands not just because he was celebrated, but because he endures. And in that, there is immense hope for artists, for dreamers, and for those who dare to tell the truth with tenderness.

The Quiet Comeback of Legacy: Why Restored Classics Are Lighting Up Our Screens Again

In an era where everything is fleeting, stories on Instagram vanish in 24 hours, TikTok trends expire before they even form memories, and the next viral reel is always a scroll away; something beautiful, almost radical, is happening in the world of cinema.

Across theatres in India and on global platforms, films like *Umrao Jaan* (1981), *Sholay* (1975), *Guide* (1965), *Pyaasa* (1957), *Charulata* (1964), *Kaagaz Ke Phool* (1959), *Chaudhvin Ka Chand* (1960), and *Sahib Bibi Aur Ghulam* (1962) are returning, not as grainy YouTube memories, but as fully restored cinematic experiences, screened as they were meant to be seen: on the big screen, in their full visual and emotional glory.

It's not just nostalgia that's drawing people in. It's reverence. And perhaps, quiet rebellion.

To restore a classic isn't just to repair scratches on celluloid or enhance the sound. It's an act of cultural conservation, a painstaking effort to retrieve the filmmaker's original vision, frame by frame, colour by colour, note by note. It's about respecting intention. And it's about time.

When *Umrao Jaan* returned to theatres this June in a breathtaking 4K restoration, complete with a re-release campaign and special screenings, it wasn't just a throwback. It was a reintroduction of elegance. The visuals, the poetry, the music, everything suddenly felt alive again, even to first-time Gen Z viewers who've never experienced a Rekha film in the theatre.

Similarly, *Sholay*, India's most iconic masala epic, was restored and screened at the prestigious Il Cinema Ritrovato Festival in Bologna in June 2025. Not just the usual version either, but the uncut original where Thakur finishes Gabbar himself, restored in full colour, with the lost climax, for the first time in decades. It marked 50 years of *Sholay* not with fanfare, but with dignity.

Meanwhile, *Guide* made its grand restored return at IFFI Goa in 2023, while *Charulata* had already been honoured in Cannes Classics back in 2013. Guru Dutt's masterpieces: *Pyaasa*, *Kaagaz Ke Phool*, and *Chaudhvin Ka Chand*, received full 4K restorations and were showcased at Cannes 2025.

In a landscape dominated by "content", not cinema, not stories, just content; the return of these films isn't just welcome. It's essential. When social media teaches us to forget fast, film restoration urges us to remember slow. It is the antithesis of the algorithm. It is memory, effort, and depth.

These restored classics are not just filling a programming gap in theatres.

They're making a statement. A statement that storytelling is not dead. That a film doesn't have to scream or trend to be unforgettable. That there is still an audience that craves weight, rhythm, and beauty in its cinema.

Think about it: a 22-year-old watching *Pyaasa* for the first time in Dolby surround, in a packed theatre, is not going for nostalgia. They're going because, perhaps for the first time, they've heard that cinema can feel like poetry. That stories can linger. That art can age, and still speak louder than ever.

This isn't just a comeback of films, it's a comeback of ideas. A comeback of deliberate dialogue, of characters with complexity, of storytelling that trusts its audience to think, reflect, and stay. These films had time. And they gave us time.

Restoration, then, is not just about past preservation. It is a mirror to the present. It asks: What are we creating today that will deserve restoration tomorrow? And more crucially: Are we even building with longevity in mind anymore?

There's something quietly subversive about screening *Charulata* today, in the same world where 10-second dance clips loop endlessly. Satyajit Ray's camera lingers on a woman peeking through lace curtains. There is silence. There is stillness. And yet, everything is happening. How rare is that kind of narrative patience now?

There's also a larger truth here. As India positions itself as a cultural and creative powerhouse, our cinematic legacy becomes a form of soft power. Restoring *Guide*, screening *Mughal-e-Azam*, reintroducing *Anand* or *Do Bigha Zamin*, these aren't just acts of reverence. They are global conversations. Statements of aesthetic confidence.

When a classic Indian film gets a standing ovation at Cannes or Bologna, it's not just a win for the past. It's a reminder to the world: We've always told good stories. Maybe we just stopped listening to them.

What restoration has done is more than just technical, it's emotional, philosophical, even political. It's brought back the soul of cinema, in an age that desperately needs it. It's reminded us that stories are not disposable. That memory matters. That beauty has its own pace.

The fact that younger generations are discovering these classics, and not as dated relics, but as living, breathing cinema; proves something profound: True stories don't age. They wait. And when they return, they don't scream for attention. They simply begin again.

So the next time you see a poster for a restored black-and-white film in your local theatre, don't walk past it. Walk into it. Sit down. And let it remind you what it means to truly watch a film. Not for a quick dopamine hit, but for something quieter, deeper, something that lingers long after the screen goes dark.

Let it teach you to wait again. To listen again. To feel again. In that dark theatre, far from the noise of trends and hashtags, you might just find something that no algorithm can serve you a story that becomes part of your soul. And that, perhaps, is where cinema begins again.

50 years of Sholay: Reinventing branding, continuity, and the immortality of Indian cinema

There are films that become hits. Then there are films that become history. And then, once in a lifetime, a film becomes Sholay.

As Sholay celebrates its golden jubilee, 50 years since it first blazed across the screens in 1975, it's not just an anniversary; it's a cultural reckoning. Very few films in the world, let alone in India, have had this kind of staying power. Half a century later, Sholay is not merely remembered; it's still quoted, mimicked, memed, revered, and restored. From dusty film reels to 4K restorations and international screenings, most recently at a special celebration in Italy earlier this year, Sholay continues to echo across generations, languages, and continents.

At its core, Sholay is everything cinema aims to be. It is not bound by genre; it is the genre. Romance, action, comedy, tragedy, emotion, revenge, sacrifice, music, values, suspense, and even a little bit of philosophy, all stitched together in perfect sync. Ramesh Sippy didn't make a movie; he created a multiverse long before the term ever existed. Jai and Veeru's friendship is legendary. Gabbar Singh is the original villain prototype. Basanti is spunky before the world used the word 'feminist.' Thakur is wrath restrained. And Radha's silence? It says more than most modern scripts ever could.

It's not hyperbole to say Sholay was ahead of its time. In fact, the industry hadn't even caught up to it until decades later.

Before marketing was a full-blown science in Indian cinema, Sholay cracked the code. Every dialogue became a catchphrase, every character an archetype, every scene a template for future filmmakers. It wasn't just a film, it was an institution in branding.

It did what today's cinema struggles to do: remain consistent in impact without constantly reinventing itself. The continuity of Sholay's legacy is its real brilliance. Every generation discovers it anew, and yet it feels timeless. Unlike other blockbusters that peak and fade, Sholay is an ever-rising curve, richer with each retelling, deeper with every revisit.

In an era where restored classics are making a quiet, powerful comeback, Sholay stands tall at the forefront. The recent high-definition restoration and special screening at the Festival Delle Culture in Ravenna, Italy, was not just a cinematic event; it was a statement. It reminded the world of India's storytelling power long before we entered the streaming wars or the Oscar circuits. Sholay being showcased internationally not as a relic, but as a masterpiece worthy of today's audience, proves its resonance. It's a living artefact of India's cinematic soft power.

Yes, we've had iconic films. Yes, we've had cult followings. But no other Hindi film has commanded the mythic devotion that Sholay enjoys. The only one to come close is Dilwale Dulhania Le Jayenge (DDLJ), which still runs at Mumbai's Maratha Mandir and inspired Switzerland's famous 'DDLJ trail.' Yash Chopra was honoured with a bronze statue in Interlaken, and iconic locations from the film remain major tourist attractions. Yet, despite DDLJ's global nostalgia and romantic appeal, the towering, all-encompassing legacy of Sholay remains unmatched.

No other Indian film has ever had a line-up like this: a classic two-hero bromance, an unforgettable villain, tragic love, memorable side characters, comedic relief, a score that lives rent-free in our minds, and moral themes that still spark conversation. All this in one movie. That too in the 70s.

In the global narrative of soft power, Bollywood has always been a quiet diplomat. But Sholay is its frontline soldier. The fact that it continues to be screened, studied, restored, and referenced internationally underscores India's ability to tell universal stories with local flavour. Whether it's the archetype of friendship, the struggle for justice, or the fearlessness of love, Sholay taps into core human emotions. You don't need subtitles to understand what Jai and Veeru mean to each other, or what Gabbar means when he says Kitne aadmi the?

And perhaps that's the secret sauce. Sholay didn't just export cinema; it exported emotion. And emotion, when done right, outlives every trend.

To revisit Sholay is not to look back with rose-tinted glasses. It is to remember what Indian cinema is capable of when every department is firing on all cylinders. From Salim-Javed's razor-sharp writing to R.D. Burman's unforgettable score, from S.M. Anwar's cinematography to the ensemble performances, it was a complete package before we even knew what a 'complete package' meant.

There's a reason we still say Yeh haath mujhe de de, Thakur or Tera kya hoga, Kaalia at parties, film schools, and street corners. There's a reason people still collect original film posters and write academic theses on its editing patterns. There's a reason it keeps coming back: restored, re-released, reloved.

Because Sholay isn't just a film, it's our memory. Our benchmark. Our cinematic heartbeat. And 50 years later, it's still our biggest, loudest, most unforgettable bang.

Not just an actor, but an era: Honouring Shah Rukh Khan's timeless brilliance

Among the celebrated names and remarkable wins, one stood out, not because it surprised anyone, but because it felt like history was finally catching up.

When the 71st National Film Awards were announced, a collective pause swept across India's cinephile community. Among the celebrated names and remarkable wins, one stood out, not because it surprised anyone, but because it felt like history was finally catching up. Shah Rukh Khan, the undisputed King of Bollywood, was named Best Actor. It wasn't just a personal victory. It was a national moment. It was a moment that struck a chord, deep and personal, for the millions who've grown up with Shah Rukh Khan on their screens, in their lives, and quite honestly, in their hearts.

For those who saw in him not just a superstar, but someone who redefined what it meant to be a man in Indian cinema: emotional without weakness, romantic without apology, powerful without aggression. So yes, the win brought joy. Immense pride. But let's be honest, there was also a quiet, unshakable thought echoing across timelines and living rooms: This should've come long ago. And yet, to say that isn't to undermine the honour itself. The National Film Awards have always stood for more than popularity; they represent craft, depth, and the cultural pulse of the nation.

Their selections are thoughtful, deliberate, and rooted in integrity. It's about recognising that sometimes, the brightest stars take the longest to be seen through a certain lens. Because when someone's brilliance is so constant, so ever-present, it can almost become invisible. And in Shah Rukh's case, that consistency, of performance, of presence, of impact, may have made his greatness feel inevitable, even taken for granted. Which is why this win means something deeper. It's not just another award in a room already full of them. It's the highest form of artistic recognition in Indian cinema. And that kind of validation? That's not just overdue.

That's historic. For a man who has shaped not just Bollywood but global perceptions of Indian storytelling, this award is more than recognition, it is an embrace from the very institution that holds cinema to its highest standards. Still, one can't help but reflect on the journey. This wasn't a sudden ascension. Shah Rukh Khan didn't become a great actor in 2023. His performances in Swades, Chak De! India, My Name is Khan, Kabhi Haan Kabhi Naa, and Devdas have long been carved into the cultural memory of this nation. These weren't just critically acclaimed films, they were transformational moments in the way we saw grief, ambition, faith, and love on screen. And yet, the National Award remained elusive.

Until Jawan. It's not uncommon in cinema for recognition to arrive at the peak of popularity or after years of consistent excellence. Amitabh Bachchan, another legend whose artistic prowess is undisputed, received his first National Award for Agneepath, not for Sholay or Deewar. Similarly, Leonardo DiCaprio won his first Oscar for The Revenant, long after The Aviator or The Wolf of Wall Street had already showcased his depth. These moments aren't oversights— they are reminders that awards, by nature, follow time and perspective. In Jawan, Shah Rukh delivered a performance that married mass appeal with sharp political commentary, emotional complexity, and technical finesse. It was action, yes, but it was also rage, fatherhood, grief, and hope.

The film held a mirror to society while keeping the audience rapt, and that balance is no small feat. In many ways, it was the perfect moment for a National Award. Because Jawan wasn't just a hit, it was a reckoning. The National Film Awards have, in recent years, shown remarkable adaptability, honouring performances that speak to India's evolving sociocultural fabric. Shah Rukh's win, then, represents a moment of beautiful convergence: a superstar returning to cinema not just with power, but with purpose, and being honoured for it in the most dignified way.

But here's another way to look at the delay: maybe this wasn't the system catching up, but a testament to Shah Rukh's own consistency. Maybe the fact that this could come even now, decades into his career, says something profound about who he is, not just as an actor, but as a phenomenon. He never stopped delivering. Never stopped surprising. Never stopped evolving. Most actors have peaks. Shah Rukh Khan has had eras. Perhaps this is what makes the award feel timely. He didn't need one defining role to prove his mettle; he had dozens. He didn't have to make a comeback to remind us of his power, he simply returned to the screen, and the world lit up again. And maybe Jawan, with its social commentary, blockbuster swagger, and deeply human story telling, was the one film that finally combined everything he's always been into one roaring, heartfelt performance.

Because Jawan wasn't just another Shah Rukh film, it was a film that felt like India was rising. And he carried it not just with star power, but with soul. This moment, in truth, transcends individual films. It marks the culmination of a career that has consistently delivered vulnerability wrapped in charisma, brilliance behind stardom, and storytelling that shaped not only the silver screen but our very sense of identity. Shah Rukh Khan was never just a superstar; he was always an actor. A powerful, intuitive, deeply emotional actor whose range was too vast to be boxed into one genre, one era, or one award.

And now, finally, the recognition has arrived, from the highest authority in Indian cinema. It came not late, but right at a time when his return to the screen felt like a homecoming. After hiatuses, health battles, shifting tides, and public silence, Shah Rukh re-emerged not to prove anything, but to remind us that legends never leave, they just wait for the perfect time to speak again.

This National Award does not define him. It simply dignifies what his audiences have always known: that he is not just a beloved icon, but a performer of remarkable depth and substance. In honouring Shah Rukh

Khan today, the National Film Awards have not just awarded a performance, they have acknowledged an era.

India will seek to shape the global AI order

When India hosts the AI Impact Summit in February 2026, it will not just be another globalmeet artificial intelligence. It is, in fact, the moment where India signals its readiness to move beyond declarations and frameworks and into the territory of delivery. After Bletchley Park, Seoul, and Paris, the global conversation has largely revolved around ethics, risk, and governance.

Now, India wants to take the baton forward, bridging aspiration with implementation, especially for the Global South.

For India, this summit is as much about positioning as it is about purpose. It strengthens India's claim of being not just a consumer of AI innovation but a creator, regulator, and exporter of frameworks. Hosting the summit in New Delhi reflects a conscious attempt to consolidate leadership, India is no longer satisfied with merely participating in the global AI order; it seeks to shape it. It also ties back to India's larger digitalstory : aadhaar, U P I , DigiLo cker, and now IndiaAI Mission, which democratize access to compute power and indigenous language models. The summit demonstrates that India's innovation narrative is not restricted to fin-tech or digital governance, it's extending to the heart of future geopolitics: artificial intelligence.

The expected outcomes of the summit are significant and wide-ranging. India is likely to push for global standards for AI protocols, focusing on creating a standardized framework for AI deployment in communication and governance. Such a framework would include interoperability, risk assessment , and ethical safeguards, ensuring that the systems shaping public life are transparent, accountable, and aligned with democratic values. Equally important will be the effort to bridge the global divide. One of the key outcomes may be a concrete roadmap enabling developing nations to access affordable AI infrastructure and datasets, addressing the Global South's long-standing complaint of being left behind in the AI revolution.

At the heart of India's contribution lies the nurturing of AI models with local roots. Open-source foundational models developed by Sarvam AI, Soket AI, Gnani AI, and Gan AI, trained on Indian languages and cultural contexts, are poised to emerge as global case studies in inclusivity. This is not just about technological sovereignty but about ensuring that AI reflects the lived realities of diverse populations. Alongside this, India's proposal to establish the IndiaAI Safety Institute through a hub-and-spoke model could set new benchmarks in risk monitoring, algorithm audits, and damage detection, making safety as central to AI innovation as efficiency.

The urgency of these outcomes becomes clearer when we consider communication. Communication is the nervous system of democracy, and if AI systems are to mediate that space, they need rules of engagement. A standard protocol for AI in communication would ensure disclosure, so that users know when they are interacting with AI-generated content. It would also demand verification, ensuring that AI-driven information is traceable and anchored to credible sources. Such a protocol would enforce inclusion, reflecting linguistic diversity, cultural nuance, and accessibility for differently-abled users. And it would demand restraint, preventing AI from amplifying hate speech, propaganda, or weaponized misinformation. To bring this vision alive, we need a phased approach.

In the short term, disclosure norms must be established, AI tools should be piloted in public service communication, and training datasets must be built across all major Indian languages. In the medium term, India must develop indigenous communication models tailored for governance, media, and education, reducing dependence on Western platforms. And in the long term, the goal should be to reimagine communication ecosystems where AI acts as a trust enabler, fact-checking in real time, preventing misinformation outbreaks, and even facilitating meaningful citizen-to-government dialogue.

The India summit is not being built in isolation; it is a direct continuation of India's stand at the Paris AI Summit in

2024, where Prime Minister Narendra Modi argued that AI must be ethical, inclusive, and human-centric. The PM stresses that while advanced nations debate future existential risks, developing countries face immediate and tangible challenge : access , affordability, and trust. He underlined that AI cannot become the monopoly of a few, and must instead serve as a tool of empowerment for all, especially in education, healthcare, agriculture, and governance. This vision now finds expression in the AI Impact Summit 2026. Where Paris was about setting out principles, Delhi is about translating those principles into practice.

By focusing on compute infrastructure, local models, and safety frameworks, India is demonstrating how ideals can turn into workable systems. It also highlights India's distinct perspective. While Western nations remain preoccupied with hypothetical "existential risks," India sees the immediate challenge as ensuring equitable AI access for farmers, students, doctors, and small businesses. The key takeaways from the AI Impact Summit 2026 will be clear. It marks India's coming of age as a standard-setter in AI governance, moving beyond the role of participant to that of global shaper. It will also cement India's role as a leader of the Global South, articulating how AI can close, not widen, the developmental gap. India's model will showcase how ethics and infrastructure go hand in hand, with GPUs, datasets, and language models standing alongside values and safeguards. Perhaps the most urgent takeaway will b e the establishment of communication protocols, because in a world mediated by A I , information in the wrong hands is as potent a weapon as any.

Finally, unlike earlier summits, Delhi 2026 will not just be about policy, but about impact, a chance to prove that rhetoric can indeed translate into results. In essence, the India AI Summit 2026 is not about showcasing technology. It is about anchoring AI to humanity's oldest and most vital function – communication. If India can strike the right balance between innovation and restraint, it won't just lead the conversation on AI. It will redefine how the world talks, listens, and connects in the age of algorithms.

Geopolitics in the Age of Scrolling: The New Language of Power and Perception

There was a time when geopolitics moved through formal rooms. A state issued a statement. A spokesperson read from a prepared text. A newspaper carried the official line the next morning. A television anchor interpreted the event for the evening audience. The world seemed to travel through a recognizable chain of authority: government, press, broadcaster, citizen. That world has not disappeared, but it has been radically dethroned.

Today, geopolitical communication no longer waits for the press briefing. It erupts through a phone screen, mutates into a meme, becomes a thirty-second reel, and is weaponized before official institutions have even finished drafting their response.

In this new environment, communication is not merely the carrier of geopolitics. It is geopolitics. The struggle between nations is no longer fought only over territory, trade routes, military alliances, energy corridors or diplomatic blocs. It is also fought over perception, framing, emotion, memory and moral legitimacy.

Traditional media has not become irrelevant, but it has lost its monopoly over first contact with reality. For many people, especially younger audiences, the first encounter with a war, coup, election, protest, climate disaster or diplomatic crisis is no longer a newspaper headline or a state broadcaster. Younger audiences are increasingly consuming news through platforms such as TikTok, Instagram, Reddit and X, placing greater trust in information from social media than older adults.

In the contemporary media environment, many newsrooms resemble theatres of geopolitical emotion. The anchor is not merely a presenter but a performer. The studio is not just a space of analysis but a stage of confrontation. Every crisis becomes a spectacle. Every disagreement becomes a shouting match. Every adversary becomes a character.

This has consequences. It simplifies complexity into combat, rewards certainty over nuance, and turns diplomacy into drama. In a tense geopolitical moment, communication can either cool the temperature or raise it. A headline can inflame. A viral clip can humiliate. A false claim can travel faster than a clarification.

This is especially critical in times of war or near-war. The battlefield is physical, but the narrative field is emotional. Governments communicate not only to inform citizens, but also to reassure allies, deter adversaries, influence neutral states, mobilize diaspora communities and shape global opinion. Earlier, strategic communication was mostly vertical: the state spoke, the media transmitted, the public received. Today, it is networked, chaotic and participatory.

One of the most fascinating developments in contemporary geopolitical communication is the rise of memes as a form of political language. At first glance, memes appear unserious. They are funny, crude, exaggerated, chaotic and often absurd. But that is precisely why they matter. Memes allow people to process events that are otherwise too terrifying, too distant or too morally overwhelming to absorb directly. They compress rage, helplessness, irony and critique into a format that travels fast.

In times of war, memes become coping mechanisms. In times of propaganda, they become counter-speech. In times of diplomatic absurdity, they become satire. In times of public grief, they become communal release.

For younger generations, memes are often not a retreat from politics but an entry point into it. They allow people to say: we see the hypocrisy; we see the cruelty; we see the ridiculousness of powerful people manufacturing crises while ordinary people pay the price. A meme can expose the emotional truth of a geopolitical situation more sharply than a formal editorial. It can puncture the inflated language of power, ridicule warmongering, mock double standards and create a sense of global solidarity among people who may never meet but recognize the same absurdity.

This is where communication becomes unexpectedly democratic. Young people across the globe may respond to the same geopolitical crisis through the same meme template. The meme becomes a tiny republic of shared disbelief. It says: borders may divide us, but the stupidity of power is universally understood.

Of course, memes can also distort, trivialize and dehumanize. They can flatten tragedy into entertainment. But dismissing them entirely would be a mistake. Memes are now part of the emotional infrastructure of international politics. They are how many people grieve, rage, resist and belong.

The social media age has also created a new diplomatic terrain: platform diplomacy. Public diplomacy campaigns are built for Instagram. Hashtags become instruments of visibility. Short videos become tools of persuasion. The old diplomatic language was cautious, layered and slow. The new digital language demands speed, clarity, emotion and shareability. A government that waits too long may lose the narrative; one that speaks too quickly may spread error or escalate tensions.

In geopolitics, narrative is not decoration. It is infrastructure. A country's narrative shapes how others interpret its actions. The same policy can be seen as aggression, leadership, self-defense, humanitarian responsibility or strategic autonomy depending on the narrative around it. The most successful geopolitical communication does not merely defend a position. It builds a worldview.

In a fragmented world, narrative coherence becomes power. Countries that cannot explain themselves are explained by others. This is particularly important for emerging powers seeking a larger global role. They must communicate not only capability but credibility, showing that their rise is constructive, collaborative and backed by institutions, innovation, culture and values.

The same platforms that democratize communication also intensify disorder. Social media can unite people across borders, but it can also flood the public sphere with fake images, manipulated videos, bot-driven narratives and coordinated disinformation. Artificial intelligence adds another danger through synthetic images, deepfake speeches, fabricated battlefield footage and AI-generated propaganda.

This is why information integrity must become central to national security and diplomatic strategy. Media literacy, trusted verification networks, responsible platform governance, ethical journalism and transparent official communication are no longer soft issues. They are geopolitical necessities.

Yet the story is not only bleak. The most powerful communication in geopolitics is not always the loudest. Sometimes it is the sentence that leaves room for de-escalation. The communication paradigm has changed permanently. Authority no longer guarantees attention. In the age of reels, shorts, livestreams and memes, attention must be earned, trust must be built, and legitimacy must be protected.

Above all, people are not passive audiences anymore. They are interpreters, critics, amplifiers and co-authors of geopolitical meaning. The age of one-way messaging is over. The age of narrative ecosystems has begun. In the end, geopolitics is not only the story of states competing for power. It is the story of humanity trying to understand itself under pressure. And communication is where that story is written, one statement, one image, one broadcast, one reel, one meme, one silence at a time.

Media Literacy and the Future of Geostrategic Communication

Conversations as part of narrative-building exercises in the geostrategic space are influenced by complex factors, identities and tools. In the day and age of instant communication, where ideas and views are churned on a 24x7 basis, narrative building and perception management suffer within the overall framework of consistency, authenticity and transparency. This is more so related to dissemination of information and messaging. Narrative building today is viewed as a stepping stone for agenda management and power equations between nations, stakeholders and entities. The challenge before narrative building in the geostrategic space is to wean off and disguise coercion through the guise of influence, content, values, non-state stakeholders and compelling yet resonating tools and ideas.

A critical element in the ecosystem is the integration and interconnect between ideas, perception, storytelling, engagement and strategic messaging, and its relationship with the role of AI in driving the narrative ecosystem. In this algorithmic age, where tools drive and judge sentiments, moods and perceptions, narrative discourse has become increasingly obsessed with tech-driven ideas, integrated with complex and diverse stakeholders and the intense push of data-driven communication.

As a consequence, the geostrategic communication space today is witnessing narrative manipulation to suit particular nations, blocs, entities and national interests. The media space contours emerging from the narrative conflict reflect a tug of war between ideas, opinions, perspectives and algorithms, leading to a confusing profile of media literacy parameters in the communication space. As opinions change instantly, thanks to the information blitz, it is critical that the foundations of media literacy remain sound, deep, robust and stable. The ability to evaluate content objectively and access information through the prism of accuracy, credibility and trust must become central to the communication ecosystem. The media literacy ecosystem should segregate information through facts, credible sources, responsible tools and strong media support structures.

The media literacy architecture is influenced by multiple narratives and instruments of information dissemination that control the language and angles of public debate, views and perceptions. Today, media literacy is subject to multiple influences and perspectives. It has to constantly battle the power of ideas and concepts that keep flowing intermittently from stakeholders at all levels.

Today, in the geopolitical space, there is an urgent need to balance communication contests that are taking place at different levels and serving several purposes. The challenge within the media literacy framework is to create proactive "communication understanding" between stakeholders, instruments of communication, national priorities, audience perceptions, national image and identity, and emerging communication interpretation. One needs to understand that the communication order is operating in a borderless world, wherein narrative-building techniques are strategically positioned and placed to influence viewpoints, communication outreach, resources, campaigns and emerging collaborations and partnerships. Hence, in 2026, it is critical that media literacy contours reinforce the foundations of communication coherence, understanding and appeal.

At the same time, the idea of national image has also become far more layered than before. It is no longer shaped only by official statements, diplomatic exchanges, press briefings or institutional communication. It is also shaped by clips, memes, influencers, explainers, podcasts, digital campaigns and citizen-led conversations. A single image, phrase, headline or edited video can travel faster than a formal clarification. This has made strategic communication more immediate, but also more vulnerable. In the geostrategic space, perception often moves before policy can be fully explained. Therefore, communication systems must not merely react to narratives after they have gained momentum. They must be designed to anticipate, interpret and respond with clarity, credibility and speed.

This is where media literacy becomes more than a civic skill. It becomes a strategic necessity. A society that can distinguish between information, misinformation, disinformation and propaganda is better placed to protect its democratic discourse and national interests. Similarly, institutions that understand the emotional, cultural and technological behaviour of audiences can communicate with greater responsibility. The goal is not only to counter falsehoods, but to create trust-based communication ecosystems where facts are accessible, public reasoning is encouraged and informed participation is strengthened.

The growing role of artificial intelligence adds another layer to this challenge. AI tools can assist in translation, outreach, sentiment mapping, content creation and audience analysis. However, the same tools can also be used to manufacture synthetic realities through deepfakes, automated propaganda, manipulated visuals, fake amplification and targeted psychological messaging. The future of geostrategic communication will therefore depend on how societies build ethical safeguards around technology. Algorithms cannot be allowed to become invisible editors of public perception without accountability. Transparency in digital platforms, responsible AI use, verification protocols and institutional preparedness will be central to protecting the information space.

The critical idea within the media literacy architecture is to design a process that understands and interprets the communication ecosystem. In the age of instant communication, a robust media literacy process will ensure a level playing field and ward off misinformation, manipulation and information malpractice. It is the strong roots of media literacy that will prevent fakery, false news and designed propaganda. As media platforms are diverse and complex, it is critical to design a process that consumes content through checks and balances of the media dissemination process.

It is a reality today that every individual is a citizen journalist. Each person is a source of dissemination, interpretation, evaluation and response. The consuming and processing information gateway is circuitous, complex and accessible on a 24x7 basis. The gateway must empower every person with skillsets to access, analyse, process, evaluate and participate in the communication discourse. The challenge therefore is to sync with the core message, understand it and interpret it.

Media literacy landscape also faces the challenges of communication diversity, participation, tech-driven content, multimedia messaging and communication symbolism. A robust media literacy framework also faces the challenges of communication fabrication, including fake news, images, deepfakes, statistical juggling and technology-influenced algorithms. Going forward, the strength of any communication ecosystem will depend on how effectively it can combine speed with responsibility, influence with ethics, and technology with trust. In the geostrategic space, the most powerful narratives will not merely be the loudest or fastest, but the most credible, consistent and rooted in public confidence.

FIFA 2026: The Rise of a New Football World

FIFA 2026 has still a long way to go, with the knockout rounds yet to be played. Nonetheless, it has already created a compelling buzz and offered unfiltered evidence of why it remains one of the biggest sporting events held globally. Every four years, we witness heightened adrenaline, rising expectations and diverse global imaginations during the football matches played. As a consequence, every edition has been characterized by the **4U's phenomenon**:

· **Unique**
· **Unprecedented**
· **Unqualified**
· **Unequivocal**

Football as a sport has undergone a strategic shift. This shift is exemplified through the upsets, victories and tenacity that audiences are witnessing globally. Football today has moved beyond being a traditional bastion of favored nations to becoming a global sporting festival. The performance of Cape Verde has created a football tsunami for pundits and strategists analyzing the emergence of a new brigade in the football fraternity. It has stunned viewers through its spectacular performance against Spain and Uruguay. DR Congo has emerged with a new killer instinct. Other nations such as Egypt, Haiti, Jordan, Uzbekistan, Iraq and Canada have also given us a whiff of professionalism that has been unprecedented and unparalleled. All this proves that the experiment to expand FIFA to 48 nations has met with success, giving new hope and aspiration to countries across the world. In the past, we witnessed the **"Mexican Wave"**, which became a natural sporting symbol at global events. FIFA 2026 has not been left behind. The tagline and narrative have echoed ideas such as **"Global Audiences Pick"**, **"Underdogs Spectacle"** and **"David V/s Goliath Contest."**

Every edition of the FIFA World Cup has given us a splash of unusual excitement, dogged performances, underrated displays and the emergence of unrecognizable dark horses. The current edition has been no exception. FIFA 2026 has so far had several defining moments, particularly through the rise of teams that were earlier seen as peripheral to the football imagination. These teams have given traditional showstoppers a run for their money. With expanded participation, football branding has also scaled new heights.

Each participating nation has given audiences a fresh taste of professionalism, along with new dynamics of skill, speed and strategy. Established superpowers have witnessed bouts of struggle and underperformance, while newer entrants have used the platform to announce their arrival with confidence. Football has transcended boundaries, leaving a lasting legacy among admirers, supporters and audiences. FIFA 2026 has shown to the world a bold new experiment, showcasing the **"Democratization of Football"** with renewed confidence, vigor and vitality.

The recent implications of FIFA 2026 have gone beyond the field of play. The enlarged format has not merely increased the number of teams; it has expanded the emotional, commercial and geopolitical footprint of football itself. With 12 groups, a new Round of 32 and the possibility of third-placed teams progressing, every match has acquired greater tactical meaning and every goal has begun to carry qualification consequences. This has made FIFA 2026 refreshing because the tournament is no longer being viewed only through the lens of traditional football powers. The entry and performance of countries such as Cape Verde, Jordan, Uzbekistan, Haiti, DR Congo and others has been received with curiosity, admiration and surprise. Their inclusion has reinforced the belief that football's future lies in wider participation, not closed dominance.

The eastern part of the world is also emerging as an important zone to watch. Asian and Middle Eastern teams are bringing discipline, speed, compact defending and fearless counter-attacking football into the tournament's mainstream imagination. Japan, South Korea, Iran, Saudi Arabia, Iraq, Jordan and Uzbekistan have shown that the football map is gradually shifting eastward. FIFA 2026, therefore, is refreshing not only because it is bigger, but because it is more representative, unpredictable and truly global.

Communication, outreach and narrative building have created new frontiers at FIFA 2026. It has been a rare symphony of diverse stakeholders leading to **"Communication Convergence."** Global conversation across multiple platforms has unleashed the power of soft power in the narrative-building process. An unusual diplomacy has emerged across stadiums, where the dynamics of sport, identity and national pride are visible in real time. We have witnessed an interconnect unprecedented in scale and volume across stadiums, players, fan communities and digital platforms. This has brought to light the importance of using sport as a medium for building a cohesive communication environment between fans, brand identity, real-time dissemination and response. All this has led to a new phase of strategic global communication, influencing national networks, global visibility and soft power connectivity. Strategic communication through FIFA platforms is reinventing narrative discourse through different tools, platforms and engagement protocols.

FIFA 2026 has shown the importance of people-centric communication and narrative building in creating a perception where sport is not limited only to playing time. It is being utilized to build bonhomie through innovative storytelling and conversations that touch the heart and emotions, rather than relying on pure statecraft alone. Audience investment has been one of the critical pillars of FIFA 2026. The emotional journey of audiences has been relayed on a real-time basis to create an impact resting on authenticity, values, aspirations and hope. Technology, value systems and emotions have together shaped the benchmarks of audience engagement and excitement. FIFA 2026 has seen a Unified Voice across stadiums, where sports lovers have chanted triumph in unison or expressed disappointment with the resolve to fight back once again. It has created "Emotional Bonding" among people through common voices, shared memories and collective sporting imagination.

FIFA 2026 has also proved to be a new "Branding Vehicle", creating a multi-layered brand platform through visual visibility, thematic positioning, FIFA logos, sloganeering, theme song placement and corporate participation. Coupled with this is the presence of iconic players such as Lionel Messi, Cristiano Ronaldo and Kylian Mbappé. FIFA has created new parameters and benchmarks for endorsements, consumer engagement and fan experiences. Loyalty, emotional participation and cultural association have become the new mantras of branding principles. Fan experiences have added to the color of branding, where the "product" is no longer just the match, but the complete universe of emotion, identity, visibility and audience acceptance created around it.

FIFA 2026 is not merely another edition of the World Cup; it is a statement on the changing geography of global football. It has shown that the sport is no longer confined to a few historic power centres, but is being shaped by new nations, new audiences, new markets and new aspirations. The expanded format has opened the gates for wider participation, while the performances of emerging football nations have given the tournament a new emotional and competitive pulse. As the world moves towards the knockout rounds, FIFA 2026 stands as a celebration of unpredictability, inclusion and global sporting democracy. It has reaffirmed that football's greatest strength lies not only in goals scored or trophies lifted, but in its power to unite identities, ignite hope and create a shared global imagination. This is the real legacy of FIFA 2026.

The New Language of Soft Power

Soft power in today's day & age of complex geopolitics has departed from the conventional nomenclature given to it. As a concept, today it is intrinsically woven into communication protocols, defining perceptions and incorporating a different interconnect with policy, outreach and narrative building. With Times the notion of soft power has drastically changed since Joseph Nye coined the term in the 1980s. While the ability to influence was limited in scope & objective earlier, it operates today in a much more complex matrix. A matrix that is outlined by new ideas, algorithms, influence, persuasion and credibility aspects. Soft power today operates within the complex architecture of state and non-state actors. Through its varied tools, the concept has become extremely dynamic, always in the search of viability, effective relationships, partnerships, consistent engagement and appeal within the parameters of national and global boundaries.

Soft power today when applied in real politics reflects deep insights, aspirations and comprehensive trust. It is no longer limited to a cultural framework alone. It has become an essential ingredient to showcase growth, progress, legacy, strategic positioning and a value system that reinforces its connection with policy, institutions and people. As a concept it has become an essential ingredient to people-centric development, governance, narrative setting and public-oriented diplomacy. While culture remains the cornerstone of soft power, it is the variations offered within the concept that has made the idea a must win input in the practice and performance of diplomacy and foreign policy. This has become more challenging in the light of the 'Digital Age' we all live in. Tech-driven growth, deeptech partnerships colours soft power through different shades and templates."

In the contemporary global order, the credibility of a nation is no longer shaped only by its economic strength or military capability. It is equally shaped by the way its institutions speak, the way its policies are understood, and the way its people are able to connect with the larger world. This is where soft power assumes a wider meaning. It becomes a bridge between domestic achievements and global recognition. It carries the ability to translate national progress into a narrative that is understood beyond borders. In this sense, soft power is not a passive asset. It is an active instrument that demands clarity, consistency and conviction. It requires countries to communicate not merely what they have achieved, but why those achievements matter for humanity, development and shared futures.

The digital environment has further multiplied the importance of this idea. Today, a policy decision, a cultural symbol, a scientific innovation, a sporting achievement or even a public campaign can travel across continents in seconds. The same speed that creates opportunity also creates vulnerability. Narratives are no longer built only through formal statements or diplomatic channels. They are built through public conversations, social media engagement, visual storytelling, influencer ecosystems, academic exchanges, diaspora networks and the credibility of institutions. Therefore, the management of soft power today requires an understanding of both substance and perception. It is not enough for a country to possess cultural depth or civilisational confidence. It must also have the capacity to present that depth in a manner that is contemporary, relatable and persuasive.

Education, knowledge and innovation have also emerged as important dimensions of soft power. Universities, research institutions, start-up ecosystems, scholarships, digital public infrastructure and technology partnerships now shape how a nation is perceived by young people, investors, researchers and policy communities. A country that is able to offer solutions in areas such as climate change, health, digital inclusion, skill development and affordable technology naturally creates goodwill. This goodwill is not artificial. It is built through usefulness, trust and the ability to contribute to global challenges. In many ways, the soft power of the present century is increasingly solution-oriented. It is not only about admiration, but about relevance. It is not only about visibility, but about value.

At the same time, cultural confidence continues to remain an enduring pillar. Languages, cinema, cuisine, literature, festivals, heritage, spirituality, yoga, traditional knowledge systems and creative industries continue to provide emotional familiarity and attraction. However, these cultural markers gain greater strength when they are connected with modern aspirations. A nation's heritage becomes more powerful when it is not presented as a relic of the past, but as a living force capable of engaging with the present. This balance between legacy and modernity gives soft power its real depth. It allows a country to appear rooted and forward-looking at the same time. It also prevents soft power from becoming ornamental, limited only to symbolic representation without strategic direction.

In this changing framework, communication has become the backbone of soft power. The language of communication must be authentic, people-centric and globally conscious. It must avoid overstatement and still carry ambition. It must be able to speak to domestic audiences with confidence and to international audiences with openness. This is particularly important because soft power rests heavily on trust. Once credibility is weakened, even strong cultural or institutional assets lose their impact. Hence, successful soft power is never built through messaging alone. It is built through the alignment of message, action and experience. What a country says, what it does, and what others experience through engagement with it must reinforce one another.

The role of diaspora communities also adds another strong layer to this discussion. Diaspora groups often become living carriers of national identity, cultural memory and professional excellence. They influence perceptions in host societies through their contribution to business, academia, technology, medicine, public life and community networks. Their success often becomes a reflection of the country's human capital and value system. When connected meaningfully, diaspora communities can create long-term bridges of trust and collaboration. They can also help translate national narratives into local contexts with greater emotional acceptance. It finally turns influence into a deeper framework of respect.

About the Authors

Chaitanya K. Prasad is a retired senior civil servant from the 1991 batch of the Indian Information Service, with over three decades of experience in public policy, strategic communication, media management, and campaign design for government programmes. As former Additional Director General, DFF, and Festival Director, IFFI, he led initiatives on stakeholder partnerships, film policy facilitation, and positioning India as a filming destination. He currently serves as Head of Promotion and Outreach, Ministry of Education, Government of India. A prolific writer and lecturer, his work spans cinema, branding, communication strategies, and geopolitical discourse.

Vaishnavie Srinivasan is a communications strategist specialising in storytelling, transmedia narratives, and impact communication. She has worked with the International Cooperation Cell, Department of Higher Education, Government of India, contributing to initiatives such as India's G20 Education Working Group and Bharat Innovates 2026. A graduate of IE Business School with a master's in Visual Media Creation and Management, she also co-authors on cinema, identity, and communication.

Zoya Ahmad is a consultant with the International Cooperation Cell, Ministry of Education, Government of India, specialising in global partnerships, education policy, and strategic communication. She leads stakeholder engagement and international policy events with G20 nations, and co-authors work on cinema and branding. Known for her creative problem-solving and transmedia storytelling, Zoya continues to foster cross-cultural dialogue and innovative communication strategies in education and media.

www.ingramcontent.com/pod-product-compliance
Lightning Source LLC
LaVergne TN
LVHW090308210926
848480LV00001B/177

* 9 7 9 8 9 0 5 6 0 7 7 3 8 *